To Be Somebody

BY EVELYN LEITE

To Be Somebody

BY EVELYN LEITE

Hazelden

First published, January 1979
Reprinted, January 1982

ISBN: 0-89486-060-7
Library of Congress Catalog Card Number: 78-060063

Printed in the United States of America

To my father for whom
understanding is
forgiveness.

For whom love is undying.

And to my family and
friends for their love
and encouragement during
my struggle to tell this
story.

Al-anon is a group of people who gather together with love to share a common problem and goal. For more information on this group write:

Al-anon Family Group Headquarters
P.O. Box 182
Madison Square Station
New York, NY 10010

FOREWORD

This is a personal document based on events which happen to people every day. They happened to me.

It is a story about alcoholism and pain, about faith and healing, and about joy and recovery. It is written that all people in the helping professions may gain insight into problems family members face when alcohol is destroying their lives. It is further written to bring love, hope, and inspiration to people trying to cope with a disease they do not understand.

Names and events are changed, but the story is real and could be happening next door to you. Or in your house.

E.L.
December 25, 1978

PREFACE

Shy and bashful, he sidled up to me. Daring and delirious, I stuck my hand in his. He was eighteen, I was sixteen. He was beautiful, I was plain. How could he notice me? He was a charmer, a dazzler. I was dull, a clod. He could disarm a whole room full of people with one lopsided grin. I could make no impression at all. He was a lover. I was a fighter. He was wild. I was controlled. He was from the wrong side of the tracks; that made him more attractive.

He had a father who alternately beat and deserted him and a mother who escaped it all by working sixteen hours a day. I had a father who alternately spoiled me rotten and held up my inadequacies for me to see, and a gentle, religious mother. He hated his parents; I scorned mine. He came from a loud, rowdy, beer drinking family. He is nothing like them. At my house no drinking or swearing is allowed; that's why my father is seldom home. I am nothing like them.

At his house, the most important thing is Possessions — underline the capital P. At my house, the most important thing is Pride, also with a capital P. He boasts about his mother making him read every word of Emily Post. I was born knowing which fork to use. He reads the funny papers. I read the news. He quit school and joined the Air Force. I struggled through. He is more fun and exciting than anybody I've ever met. I am more daring and willing than anybody he's ever met. Together we laugh uproariously at the world. He makes me feel like a princess. I would have licked his boots. We flout everybody's objections to our relationship.

Heaven is the day we get married.

Hell is the year after, and after, and after.

Daddy cried at my wedding.

One

Unable to sleep, I lay propped on my elbow, my hand cupping my face. Warm with the experience of the peak of love, I watch Harold, my Adonis, sleep. My eyes soak up his curly hair, his handsome face, his innocence in sleep, his lean muscular body. On his side, one leg bent, one arm out-stretched, he looks like a runner for the eternal flame. Silently I congratulate myself for having the good fortune to be married to such a man. "God," I say, "thank you for sending me this goodness, this new beginning. I will do my best to deserve it. Please forgive me for not making it to church anymore. I promise to try to do better."

Young and healthy and full of wonder at the joy we find in each other, we are two kids let loose in Disneyland. Laughing, playing, drinking, dancing and taking all the thrill-spilling rides. One sophisticated Air Force man and one country bumpkin, three thousand miles away from home. No money, no car, no home of our own. But who cares. We have each other. When food runs out, we go to bed and concentrate on other things. This is the beginning, this is the start of a life that will know no equal.

It's a lot more fun to go out drinking and dancing than it is to go to school. I'm free from home, free from them. I can do whatever I want with Harold. Nobody hollers if the refrigerator door hangs open; nobody says shut off the lights. Nobody tells me how insufficient I am; nobody says I'm dumb.

I am relaxed and secure in the knowledge that I have made it to my ultimate destiny, that of being MRS. SOMEBODY.

Harold is my husband, my lover, my friend, my father, my brother, my life. That lopsided grin destroys me, pulls out my gut. I am his to have, to own, to love.

My excitement runs rampant when he walks in the door. No is not in my vocabulary or in his. It's "yes, darling," "yes, love," "hey, babe, let's do it." Wild and free, heedless and hasty, we taste and take. Rebellious and humble, we live for the moment. Tomorrow will take care of itself. For now it's enough to be together, to be on our own, to live our lives for each other. We spend our last dollar on a pitcher of beer. I worry about that; no, I don't. Harold is the man of this house, the boss. It's his dollar.

I push to the back of my mind any unsettling thoughts that try to creep, to worm their way to the surface, and think of the promised "happy ever after." I will be soft, compliant, and pure. There will be no need for unpleasant bickering in this house, no cutting remarks, no searing the soul. Love will conquer all.

Harold calls me his "old fashioned girl," and teases me about my puritan background. He loves it because he had to teach me how to make love. Sex at our house is not taboo. Nothing at our house is taboo. I am his wife, his mistress, his mother, his maid, his laundress, his bookkeeper.

Two

But sometimes there are questions.

This is what marriage is all about? Cooking, cleaning, making beds? Is this all there is? What am I supposed to do while Harold is at work all day? I whip through the house work or ignore it for a good book. Then I wait, wait for Harold to come home and the fun to begin.

Harold must never know what I have discovered; I will hide it so well he will never find out. It will be my own guilty secret that I hate housekeeping, cooking, and coffee klatches. In fact, the only thing I really like about marriage, other than Harold himself, is sex. God forbid he should ever find that out. Sex is for him; not for me, as he let me know so gently.

The merry-go-round is beginning to get boring. I make excuses for a lot of Harold's behavior because of the difference in our backgrounds. I know that with quiet persistence I can change him. I think it is time to settle down, start building a life, a savings account. "Harold," I tell him, "let's stay home tonight. Maybe we can even get up and go to church in the morning."

"Aw, come on, beautiful, loosen up, let's have some fun. I promised the guys we'd be there." Or, "Hey, beautiful, I am the man in this family, and I want to show you off."

And because no one has ever called me "beautiful" before, and because I can't stand to see Harold's face downcast or disappointed, I loosen up and we have some fun. Harold dances a jig and his face lights up like a prism in the sun when he gets his way. I can't stay upset with him even when I try.

In my family, whoever can say, laughingly, the most ego busting remarks wins. I learned early in life how to cut the soul, cripple the ego with a glance and a well-aimed, well chosen word. In fact, it seems to me my only talent, one I groomed and polished to stay even with my father and four brothers. I am the champion, but I don't want to win that way. Besides it's lots easier not to cross Harold. At least for me; everyone else can do it.

I don't understand Harold's reticence to stick up for himself against other people. Not that he has to often, his charm usually gets him through most situations. But to let the telephone man, the landlord, the neighbors take advantage of him? Where is his gumption, where is his spunk? If there is a battle to do, I am the one who does it. He always cheers me on saying, "Go get 'em, tiger. What do you think I married you for?" It makes me feel like a power house, but sometimes I wish he would take over so I could be the one that is charming. When I try to explain to Harold that I don't like the "he's a nice guy, but his wife is a bitch" feeling I get from this, he won't talk about it.

Three

"Nagging, nagging, always nagging." Why is Harold screaming at me? I just asked him to make a decision on whether or
not we could afford to buy some new curtains for this old
place. "If you want new curtains, buy new curtains. You're
the one with the checkbook."

"But, Harold, I need to know if that is what you want. I'm
tired of looking at this dump. Maybe we should move."

"Okay, we'll move, If you want to move, we'll move."

"Harold, please, I just want you to make the decision."

"Jesus Christ, my decision is to go for a beer." He grabs his
coat and leaves in a huff. I am bewildered; how did that
happen? Was I being unreasonable? Yes, I guess I was; you
can't expect a man to care about curtains and that was a nasty
crack about the "dump." He can't help it if we don't make
much money. Maybe if I go to work that will help. That's it, I
can get a job.

But the checkbook, I don't want the checkbook. I have tried
several times to give it back but nothing gets paid, nothing gets
done, and the money disappears. He always hands it back with
a sheepish grin, "I'm sorry, babe; guess I'm just no good at
figures." I resent this a lot especially when I have to juggle a

too-small income twice as much to fit in what he missed, but I don't say anything. I am proud he needs me, proud I can do something he can't.

I have lots of mixed emotions about Harold lately. On one hand I feel loved and powerful; on the other I feel used and tired. I try to talk these feelings over with Harold but he won't talk. He says he will let me know when I do something wrong and he does. Sometimes when I insist, he sits down and says, "Okay, talk." And then he either retreats into his own little world while I talk and he listens, or he says, "Hey, hey baby, it's not like that," and decides to make love right in the middle of my most profound statements. It doesn't take him long to convince me that his idea is better than mine. I tell myself that I am making a big deal out of nothing, nobody could be kinder or sweeter than Harold, except sometimes I wish he would talk to me more.

I will make the decisions if that's what he wants. I will stop nagging if nagging is what it is. I will work on my personality until Harold is happy. I will be the best wife that ever walked. I will take care of the checkbook and I'll be more careful about cracks about money. "God," I say, "sometimes I don't mean to say the things I do, they just pop out. Please help me to be a good person, a good wife. Help me to make Harold happy. Help me to get him to church."

"Harold, today is my birthday."

"I know, babe, Happy Birthday,"

Is that all, Happy birthday? No party, no horns, no cake, no presents? No flowers, no notice, just "I know"? "Harold, at our house we always make a really big deal out of birthdays, better than Christmas even."

"Yeah, I see you got about six packages in the mail today. What more do you want?"

Hurt is not the word for the way I feel. If I have to tell him what more I want, then I don't want it. Whoever heard of having to ask for a birthday present? At Christmas it is the same. I sit for hours and glare at him. It was so much fun planning and shopping and hiding and wrapping. But all the presents under the tree are for Harold. "I'm sorry, babe, I didn't have any money." Harold wouldn't think of giving me a gift that cost less than $50.00, therefore I get nothing at all. I am embarrassed to tell my friends. What will they think of me?

"Harold, why is it that every time we get in a serious discussion you refuse to discuss it? Why is it that every time I get angry you slam out the door? Why can't we ever just sit down and talk things over?"

"Listen to me, babe," Harold says, "I am not good with words the way you are, and besides, whatever you want I want." Harold sits with his shoulders hunched, a beguiling look on his face. I go to him and lay my head on his shoulder.

"Harold, look at me; maybe you're happy with the way things are but I'm not. We need to get some things settled; we have to talk about bills and feelings and things."

"Goddammit, babe, leave me alone. I am sick and tired of your worrying. What do you want from me anyway?"

To the slamming door I scream, "I want you to stand up to me, I want you to be a man, I want you to talk to me. I'm tired of having to carry the whole load!" Collapsed in sobs, I wait; he will be back, he always is, and he will be sorry and contrite and I will ask him to forgive me as usual. I will just have to try harder.

Money is getting tighter and tighter. Harold's Air Force pay just doesn't go around. To make matters worse, one pay day he comes home with a new watch and a pearl ring for me. Two things I have been wanting for a long time. "To make up for your birthday, babe, and for Christmas."

"Oh, God, how can I get mad at a guy like that?" I try to be grateful, but the rent is due, the bills are piling higher and higher and I am seven months pregnant.

Four

We have to move to a cheaper apartment; the new baby is going to need so many things that we can't afford. Humming and singing up on a chair, I am putting things away. We had to buy a lot of things today that we can't afford but I am delighted with what we got. Harold is in the other room trying to assemble the new crib. He comes out, "Why are you up on that chair? Get down before you hurt yourself."

"Harold, I'm all right. You mind your business and I'll mind mine; I'll be careful."

"Goddammit, I said get down!" He jerks me viciously to the floor. It hurts my back.

"You son of a bitch!" I scream. "Leave me alone; that hurt."

Slap, across the mouth; slap again! He is shaking me, "Don't ever call me that, not ever. Do you hear?"

"Okay, Harold," I sob, "I won't, I'm sorry."

When Brian is born, Harold is thrilled and delighted — an arrogant, loveable, boastful braggart. I am scared to death and worried sick about my ability to handle this new situation, totally in awe of this miracle. I try to discuss it with Harold, but he shrugs it off and gives his usual answer to my thoughts,

"That's all right, babe, you can handle it."

Now it is Brian who makes me feel like a million dollars. Nobody in my whole life has ever so single mindedly preferred me over anyone else. I don't have to lift a finger to get his love, it is just there. I'm dizzy with sinless pleasure over my small son and overwhelmed with the responsibility placed in my hands. I begin to have fears, uncontrollable, crawling, crushing fears. One of my relative's baby died in its crib. I worry about the same thing happening to Brian and check him constantly. I worry about something happening to Harold, leaving us alone and destitute; I worry about something happening to me, leaving Brian without a mother.

To appease a God I fear, I make bargains, small promises, big promises, anything. I promise God to be a good mother, a good wife, a better neighbor. I will deny myself the things I want the most. Harold refuses to listen to my fears and gets angry if I mention them. He is superstitious. "You keep fooling around, babe, and you'll make something happen."

Harold is jealous of his own son. I try to understand it but I fail. Surely he can see how very special he is, surely he loves him as much as I do. How could he not? I read all the books on what to do with new fathers, but nothing I do seems to work. Against my will and better judgment, I leave Brian with a babysitter, sick or well, and continue to party with Harold. The more fun I have, the guiltier I feel.

I can see Harold fighting against his jealousy and losing the battle.

"Keep him quiet."

"Shut him up."

"Let him cry."

"Leave him alone." Yet he wants everyone to see him, his small son he's so proud of fathering. He takes his turn petting him and caring for him, but his jealousy crops up in small ways. Accidentally stepping on his fingers when Brian is crawling on the floor. Pulling his hair. Throwing him in the air until he screams in terror, then putting him down in disgust as if to say "See, he's not so much."

He sets things in front of Brian, allowing him only to look, slapping his fingers if he reaches. I am constantly in the middle screaming, fearing, angry, confused. I resolve to keep Brian out of Harold's way. I burn with silent, hateful resentment when he *accidentally* knocks him over, *accidentally* pinches his fingers, and deliberately punishes him for infractions of **his** rules.

"I want him to be tough, babe," he says, "you've got to be tough to make it in this world."

Yet, even as I hate the roughness, the smallness of it all, I feel pain and hurt for Harold. Pain for his past that makes him like this. Hurt for his hurt. I hate being in the middle, forced to be protector, restrainer, peacemaker, fixer of hurts.

"Hey, babe, some of the guys asked me to join a bowling league. Can I?"

"Harold," I'm exasperated, "if you want to join a bowling league, join a bowling league! Why ask me?"

"Because you have to give me the money."

"Harold, when are you going to start asking me if you can go to the bathroom? You ask me everything else."

"Harold, is this all the money there is left? Where did it go?"

"Well, babe, I had to buy a new bowling ball, and I can't bowl without shoes, and I needed the bag to carry them in."

"But Harold, how are we going to manage?"

"Look, don't bitch at me. I asked you and you said it was all right. How the hell do I please you anyway?"

By the time Brian is eight months old, I can no longer avoid going to work; things are getting tougher all the time. Both our parents have to bail us out periodically with loans and it is getting very embarrassing. Early one morning a friend and I go job hunting, leaving Harold to baby-sit. It is a long, tiring day filling out applications, knocking on doors and taking tests, but at 5:30 we return surprised, exhausted, weather beaten, consumed, and triumphant! I can't wait to tell Harold. It's a good job in a factory, better money than I've ever made. I am thrilled with it. Harold greets me at the door, "Where the hell have you been? I've been worried sick."

Harold, you knew I was going job hunting, and listen to this, I GOT A JOB"

"Oh yeah, is that supposed to make me happy when you've been out running around all day leaving your baby alone? Now tell me the truth, goddammit. It doesn't take this long to find a job. Who have you been screwing around with?"

I know he is upset because his wife has to work, but does he have to talk that way? I apologize, console, cajole. Anyway he took good care of Brian; he is sweet and clean and gurgling.

Everyday I take Harold to the base, Brian to the baby-sitter, and drive seventeen miles to work. But, thank God, we are getting out of the hole and life is much easier, even though the Air Force sends Harold away for three months, and he doesn't send us a penny. By the time he comes home, I have us almost even with the board. I really like working even though the house work piles higher and higher. "Harold," I say, "why can't you help sometimes? I work just as hard as you do."

"Goddammit," he says, "don't tell me how hard I work, you don't know how hard I work." So it piles higher. I decide that if Harold wants his uniforms ironed he can damn well iron them himself. He does, and if the neighbors happen to drop in while he is doing it, they give us a hard time. If it's women, they ooh and ah over what a good husband he is, praising him to the skies. If it's men, they tease and cuss and tell Harold he's making them look bad. Privately I wish they would all mind their own business, and wonder why Harold doesn't throw the iron at them.

Being in the Air Force is like being in a large family. Friends drop in, we booze it up, but no one can afford to go anywhere. We have a special closeness that exists from everyone having the same kinds of problems; money and uncertainty about where we will be next are the two major ones. Everybody cheers for somebody "getting out" and agonizes or celebrates with someone being transferred. We all speak the same language, using terminology and slang peculiar to the Air Force.

I have learned to expect the unexpected with Harold. My way to self-preservation is sex and the silent treatment. I can go for weeks without talking to him about anything more than the weather. It's easier not to make waves. Sex is withdrawn or rewarded depending on how well he treats me. Not without a fight, but I'm cool, resolute.

Five

One afternoon Harold rushes home excited, stimulated, looking like a small boy with his head in the clouds. "We can go
home: not home, but close to home. I can get transferred, but
I have to tell them right now. What should I do?"

"Is it a good opportunity? Would you like it better there?
When do we have to leave?" I am as impetuous and excited as
he. We have four days to pack up and sixty dollars to get three
thousand miles. That's o.k., we can do it. It's fun and
exciting.

At our new base, housing is hard to find. We end up in the
slums in the city. I am scared to death twenty-four hours a
day. We have been here three weeks. I haven't been on the
base yet, and I haven't met anybody here. Every time I want to
do something or go somewhere or say anything, Harold
doesn't feel good. I know he is faking it. Why is he acting so
ornery? My next door neighbor, whom I have only said hello
to over the clothes line, knocks on my door. She is excited,
"Are you Mrs. M---?"

"Yes."

"Your husband is in the base hospital, the doctor wants you
out there right away." How? I don't have a car! She doesn't

have a car! I just barely know where the base is. I rush over
and use her phone. The doctor says Harold has a perforated
ulcer and may not live more than a few hours. I ask if the
ambulance can come and get me; they say no. I don't know
what to do. Think, dummy, don't just stand here while your
husband dies. Do something! What? I go back and finish
scrubbing the floor I was in the middle of when she came. My
mind is frantically searching, thinking, wondering. I remember
one name of one guy Harold has mentioned. I know he is a
staff sergeant. I run next door to use the phone. Right! Here it
is, Sergeant Aims. Frantically I dial the phone, "God, let
somebody be home." I am in luck! To the voice that answers I
say, "Mrs. Aims, you don't know me, but . . . ." She comes
right away and we rush to the hospital. Harold is out of
surgery. Only time will tell if he will live. I sit night and day by
his bed praying. God hears me.

While Harold is recuperating, we go to stay with my folks,
giving up our apartment and storing our few possessions. I
never see him while we are there. He spends most of his time
sitting in a bar with his brothers. I'm worried sick. Drinking
with ulcers! Is he trying to kill himself? I plead, I nag, I
accuse, I switch tactics and baby him, waiting on him hand
and foot, catering to his every need. Finally, thank God, it is
time to go back to the base. My dad and Harold do the same
damn things, and yet my dad is blasting me all the time about
Harold. "He's no damn good," he says, "why don't you
make him shape up?"

"Me, is it my fault?"

"I wouldn't doubt it," he says, "you're just as damn ornery
and stubborn as he is, maybe worse."

"Dad," I say, "why don't you like Harold?"

"Aw," he says, "I don't dislike him, but the son of a bitch
hangs out in the bar every night. And you, you're always
running after him, leaving your poor mother with a little baby
to take care of."

"Where did I learn to drag people out of bars?" I ask

bitterly, thinking how I have been dragging him home for years. "He is no different from you. You hang out in the bar every night."

He jumps up from his chair red-faced and angry, eyes blazing with fury. Grabbing his hat he heads for the door. "Oh, yes," he says, "you think everything he does is alright, don't you? Well, I don't have to stay here and listen to this. Maybe Harold has the right idea, anything to get away from you."

"Oh, yeah!" I scream. "If you want a drink, you've got a bottle in the closet. You stay here, I will leave!" Speechless, he glares at me, the hatred in his eyes reflecting the hatred in my own. "Dad, please . . . ." My words trail off as the door slams and I am talking to an empty room.

He always was and still is my hero. What is wrong with me that I can't make him see that? I stand there hopelessly staring at the door as mom walks in. She is tired and worn, "What was that all about?" she says.

"Oh, just the same old thing." I say resigned and hopeless.

I can't wait to get out of here! Harold would do anything to please my father. "Give up," I say, "I have been trying all my life."

Back at the base we stay with Sergeant and Mrs. Aims until we can find a house. This time we buy an old, beat up trailer home. One hundred dollars down and two hundred dollars a month for life. That salesman saw us coming. Nothing worked, pipes were broken, wiring shot. Harold won't say anything. We live without water or electricity until I finally scream that if he doesn't fix it, I am leaving. "Go," he says.

Go I do, back to my parents. When I say I'll take Brian and the car, that he can have the trailer house and the bills, he fixes it. About time. One more week with my father and I will commit mayhem.

By the time Brian is two years old I am pregnant again and sick. Something is going wrong. The doctors don't understand my headaches and swollen body. My constant bleeding weak-

ens me and the essence of terror eats and sleeps with me.
Harold will not accept my weakness. It is as if he can't
function. I try not to let him down, I look at other pregnant
women and think if they can do that, I can, too. I can't. I end
up in the hospital, time after time, until the doctor says after
the fifth trip that I have to stay in bed and not lift a finger.
Harold takes Brian to a baby-sitter resentfully, clumsily tries
to cook, refuses to wash a dish or sweep a floor. "I cannot
stand lying in this mess any longer!" I scream.

"Then clean it up!" he screams back. I do.

Harold takes Brian to the baby-sitter, goes to work,
sometimes comes home and sometimes doesn't. I can't stand
to have Brian gone all day, let alone all night.

"Harold, if you are going to go out in the evening, please
bring Brian home first."

"Then you won't let me go!" he spits at me.

"Yes I will, darling, I won't say a word." So Harold brings
Brian home and goes out by himself while I sit home festering
like an open wound, sharpening my tongue. Always a master
at a razor sharp jab to the ego, I outdo my own best efforts.
Harold responds with a slamming door.

Six

Lying in the delivery room, moaning with anguish and praying out loud, I deliver twins, terminating my six month pregnancy. Bloody and frightened, I beg for their lives. Somebody says, "Give her a shot and shut her up."

When I wake up, Harold is sitting by the bed crying. The babies are still alive but it doesn't look good. I know when I see the doctor and the nurse coming down the hall with the minister what they are going to tell us. I try to run. My life depends on not hearing what they have to say; but they catch me by the window. I put my hands over my ears to shut out their words. The babies are dead! I don't eat, I don't sleep, I don't function. My only thought is to get home to Brian. Nothing must happen to him.

I am crippled, my soul is crippled. To see someone with a new baby sends me into spasms of icy infernos. In my bed I sob for hours. Harold spends most of his time comforting me, trying to heal my wound. When I am able to travel, he takes us on a trip. At the motel, he goes for a package of cigarettes and forgets to come back all night. I'm crushed but not mad. The way I've been acting, I deserve it.

After the trip, I'm in a frenzy to relieve this miserable,

overpowering feeling of inadequacy as a person, wife, mother. Most of the time I feel like I am outside my skin watching myself; criticizing, nagging, censuring my own behavior. The pressure leaves me disoriented, bumbling, clumsy. With a desperate desire for diversion, my body and my hands scrub, clean, purge the house of every speck of impurity. My mind watches laughing because I can't do the same for my soul.

Harold and I go on a shopping binge, charging things we can't afford to remodel the house. Carpet, lumber, ceiling tile, furniture. We tear into the project with obsession, ripping out walls as if they were the enemy. When the project is completed after months of hard work, I'm beginning to feel like a whole person again. Only one thing really bothers me, Harold's refusal to work any other shift than midnight to 8:00 a.m. I am scared to death to stay alone and often stay awake all night listening for noises, afraid to go to sleep for fear of waking up dead. Harold shrugs off my fears refusing to listen, refusing to work days.

As promotion time rolls around in the Air Force and Harold is passed over for the third time, he begins to go to work sloppy and unkempt, and drinks beer, lots of beer, in front of the TV. Bitter and unrelentlessly angry, he puts in for a transfer. "If we would just get away from this place, every-thing would change. I just can't work for that squirrelly little bastard" (his supervisor). "It's all his fault I didn't get promoted; he doesn't like me."

I'm beginning to notice that everything that happens is either my fault, Brian's fault, or someone else's fault, but never his. I tell him if he would have deserved a promotion he would have gotten it.

"It's about time you grew up, little boy." Harold hates it when I call him "little boy." I do it often.

Harold had to re-enlist to get his transfer but he got it. Now, instead of being five-hundred miles away from home, we will be across the ocean in another country. Harold has to go ahead and leave me behind. Privately I'm glad to see him go. (I feel guilty as hell about this feeling.) I move home to stay with my mom and dad and go to work to pay up all the bills Harold left behind. He sends no money, and the house is repossessed before I can sell it.

Harold has been gone for eight months. Brian and I have a small apartment near my folks. Being single is fun; I live for Brian and my job. I work long, hard hours but the raises and promotions come fast. It's a challenge to do a better job each day than I did the day before. Sometimes I get a little lonesome for Harold, especially since he never writes, but it's really exciting to be a career girl.

I try to get along with dad but he is so changeable, and I constantly alternate between wanting to kill him and wanting to take care of him. One minute he is angry and abusive, the next he is pleading and apologetic. He smothers Brian and me with attention, then he ignores us. Drunk or sober, he always knows what is best for me and it is always the opposite of what I am doing.

Mom is in the middle placating, explaining, listening. She tells me he doesn't even remember half the things he says. I find it impossible to believe anybody could be so rotten and not remember it. How can she be so calm, so patient, and how can he treat her the way he does? I think of all the years she has stayed home alone, all the things she has had to do without, all the excuses she makes for him. I think of the time she almost died from a bursting ulcer, he sat by her bed day after day praying and telling me over and over, "God won't let her die, she's too good." When we brought her home — when we brought her home, he got drunk.

When I tell Harold that I've decided not to move over there at all but wait for him here, I get bombarded with letters, sometimes two a day. "Please come over. I can't live here without you. I promise everything will be different. I'll do anything you say, I'll talk to you, I won't drink, I won't lose my temper. . . . "

From Harold's commanding officer, "Harold has come to

me with this problem and since it's affecting his work . . . .''

From the chaplain, "I am sure you and Harold can work out your problems if you stay together. Think of your vows. You don't have the right to do this to your child . . . .''

As I pack up my suitcase, I say to Brian, "Due to popular demand and your mother's gutless guilt, we are going to go live with your father.''

Over there Harold is full of delight, dancing around, promises spilling out of his mouth, dozens of presents for me and Brian. I wonder how I could have ever not wanted to be with him. Two days after our arrival, Harold leaves on a Saturday morning to buy groceries; he doesn't come back until Sunday. Stuck in a strange house, in a strange country, no friends, no family, no money, no job, I contemplate suicide for the first time. When Harold does come home he rants and raves about how if I wouldn't have given him such a bad time about coming over he wouldn't have stayed out all night. With my eyes wide in a violent struggle of disbelief his fist comes crashing into my face.

Harold sits around sober, downcast and contrite. "Harold, I'm going to tell you this just once. If you ever hit me again I will call the APs (Air Force police) and I will get you busted, court martialed if I can.'' He doesn't hit me again, he throws chairs, tips over tables, and puts his fists through the wall.

. Life in Japan is tiresome and boring. American women aren't allowed to work. I am homesick, lonesome and broke. Once in a while Harold and I go out to see the sights and those days are fun but few and far between because we don't have a car. I join the church and teach Sunday school. Brian and I trudge to church every Sunday morning, with or without Harold. On the days Harold comes with us, we have a lot of fun messing around the base, eating dinner in the airman's club. On days when he hasn't been home all night and I don't know where he is, it takes a superhuman effort to get through a Sunday school class.

I check stacks of books out of the library and embark on a

self-improvement campaign. I study and write, and write and study and work out schemes to gain more knowledge. Harold tears up my papers and throws my books around. When someone comes to see us and asks about the stack of books and papers he says they are his. I don't tell anyone any different, I want him to look good.

I make a few friends over there, but I don't work at it. Harold's two best buddies become my buddies because they practically live at our house. They keep me company while Harold is drinking, drive me to the store, play with Brian and buy me presents. Harold is furious over this and begins to either stay home or take them with him when he drinks. All three of us work on him to quit drinking.

One of Harold's buddies starts getting very suggestive and finally tries to seduce me, even though I am now pregnant and he knows it; I throw him out. I don't tell Harold, but I can feel him knowing why the "buddy" doesn't come around any more and blaming me for it.

The other buddy remains loyal and faithful; many times he picks up the pieces, arbitrates and loans Harold money. Pete is always there. Sometimes I want to scream "Leave us alone!" but he is so good and kind, and the misery in his eyes when he looks at me stops me from saying it. Harold sees it too, and on his good days he teases me about being a pregnant seductress. I laugh because I'm flattered and because Pete has the same appeal for me as a reliable old sheep dog.

Two weeks before the baby is due, Harold staggers in three hours late with a guy from work and announces he is only after the money in Brian's bank. He is going downtown to a bar. I follow him into our bedroom and beg him not to go. "Harold, you don't even like that guy, why do you want to drink with him?"

"Shut up, you slut, leave me alone! I said I'm going and I'm going! I don't give a damn if you are pregnant. It's probably not even my baby!" With a well aimed shove he sends me sprawling on the bed and walks out. The next minute he is back, gripping my chin with his hand like a vise. He grabs my hair and yanks, waving a handful of my hair in my face he says, "Don't you lock the door either, you goddamn bitch; do you hear me? Do you hear me?"

Stunned and disbelieving I sit and stare at the hair in my lap. The door slams. Suddenly, savagely, I go wild. With a strength born of fury, I whip through his closet tearing everything I touch. Shirts, pants, buttons go flying. When there isn't a whole piece of clothing left in the closet, I start on the dresser drawers, knocking them on the floor in my frenzy. Like a mad woman, I hurl the radio at the door, the alarm clock follows. Breaking and smashing everything within reach, I am a wrathful witch foaming at the mouth.

I feel Brian tugging at my hand, "What's wrong, mommy?" He's sleepily rubbing his eyes.

"Oh my God, what have I done? I've got to get out of here. What a terrible mess; Harold will kill me. Brian, sweetheart, we have to go stay with a friend tonight, you put on your clothes while mommy runs down the street and calls a cab. I'll be right back, baby, o.k.?"

We stay for three days at the friend's house. Tearfully apologizing, Harold comes after us. My friend is so sorry for Harold, he is so downcast and contrite. Between her and Brian I don't have a chance.

Eric is born. He comes screaming and protesting into the world late one afternoon. He is sick a lot and nothing makes him happy. His illness only makes him more precious to me. His fussing only gives me more reason to hold him. Walking the floor with him at night is infinitely more satisfying than pacing it alone. Daily, nightly and in between I thank God for letting me have him. Brian is not happy with all the attention this fussy, complaining foreigner gets. I refuse to leave him with a baby-sitter I don't know, so Pete takes my place walking the floor with Eric when Harold and I go shopping or to the movies. I don't want to go but they make me.

One night Eric is really sick, struggling to breathe. His

strangling, raspy cries frighten me. The nearest phone is a block away. I run to it and call all over the base trying to find Harold; everywhere I leave frantic messages for him to come home. Pete gets the message. Pete comes and rushes us to the hospital. Later, when we are home, Harold comes in bumbling drunk and antagonistic. "How dare you make me look like a fool! How dare you, you bitch! Do you know what that looks like, having another man take your wife and baby to the hospital?"

"Harold, I couldn't help it, I couldn't find you." Pete is sitting there, eyes downcast, his body trying to chameleon itself into the woodwork. I don't want to embarrass any of us any more, so I go to bed with Brian and Eric. Harold and Pete spend the rest of the night drinking.

The next day I go to Harold's commanding officer. I am so embarrassed I think I am going to be sick, but heart in throat, hands shaking, I tell him I have to be sent back home. He doesn't force me to say too much, but mostly looks sympathetic. I want to scream at him to forget the sympathy, I don't need it and I don't want it, but I can't. In five days I'm on my way home.

Seven

Life at home with my two sons is, for the most part, quiet and happy. I work, I read and I dream a lot. I have a burning desire to be free. Free, what a heavenly word. I dream about a life without Harold and it's like flirting with demonic desires, because my mind won't accept it. My thoughts run amuck. How could I do that to Brian and Eric? Isn't half a father better than none? You can't get a divorce, you married him for better or for worse. He is sick. You wouldn't leave him if he had a physical problem. Divorce is a sin. Do you want to rot in hell? The guilt I feel for even wanting to be rid of him is overpowering.

My family tries to understand what I am going through. I don't tell them anything. My father travels between having the best grandchildren in the world, the lousiest son-in-law and the stupidest daughter. My mother and brothers say little and quietly support me. Feeling a need to get clear away, I move to California with a friend who has just inherited her dead sister's three kids, and whose fiancé lives in California. The seven of us make quite a sight as we pull out of town, the car loaded to the hilt, luggage rack, crib, stroller and high chair tied on the top with ropes.

California is rough, money is tight, jobs can't be had, food is scarce, the furnished house we rent is run down and hopeless. It is all part of the adventure. All the kids are in school, except Eric, and we take him with us to see the sights and enjoy the California sun. We sell things we can spare, cheat the landlord every chance we get and keep our friendship tight by cheering each other along.

A letter came from Harold today; he is getting out of the service ten months early. I have to drive six hundred miles to meet his plane to the clearing base for people leaving or coming into the country. When he gets off the plane, I am going to tell him to go home without me. I will deal with my conscience later. As he walks toward me, I see his handsome face downcast and pale. He walks slow, his sleeve is bare, no stripes — busted! My husband got busted, shipped home in disgrace. I couldn't leave him now, he needs me. Brian is beside himself with joy at seeing his father; he wraps himself around his legs and holds on for dear life.

Harold doesn't have much to say about his missing stripes. I can tell he's really hurting. Quiet and subdued, he waves away the whole thing with a sentence or two about how somebody else did something he got the blame for. I don't pursue it. I'm hurting for him.

Harold has been a "civilian" for three days. We are home; he has to drive back the six hundred miles for the final act of signing the papers and collecting the last pay check. While he is gone, Eric is fussy and feverish. One morning his temperature is too high, and I have a neighbor drive us to the base hospital. In the emergency room he gets a check-up and a shot. The neighbor takes me home and leaves to go downtown. Eric is not getting better. His fever has to come down, so I take off all his clothes and wrap him in a wet bath towel. He goes into convulsions. Running down the highway with a naked baby in my arms, my clothes dripping wet from the towel, I flag down a car to take me back to the base.

The doctors don't know what is wrong with Eric. They're

frantically running tests, and they tell us he may not live. They decide he has spinal meningitis, picked up from the Air Force base.

Harold and I sit by his bed, afraid to leave him for a minute for fear he will slip away from us. A week goes by, I sit there and hold his hand and bargain with God. "Please, God, don't let him die. Please, if you will just let Eric live, I will be the best wife and mother in the whole world. I promise I'll never think about divorce again. Oh God, if you are trying to punish me, please do it some other way. Please don't take Eric." He hears me! He hears me! "Oh thank you, God, you won't be sorry. I'll prove it to you. I'll be better and I'll make Harold be better too, you will see."

Harold half-heartedly looks for a job. He doesn't find one, but he doesn't drink either. We have a little money from his mustering out pay so Harold decides to go to school. I can work, he says. "What do you mean," I say, "I've been looking for a job for months." Fearing for all our survival, I insist we take what money we have and head for home.

Eight

The doctor's office is crowded and stuffy with yellow peeling walls. The only adornment is a picture of Christ's face hung from an oversized nail sticking out of a large vertical crack. A straight-backed wooden chair sits next to a dusty desk; disheveled papers lie strewn on top and an overflowing ash tray sits in the middle. Crammed in a corner is a black leather reclining chair taking up most of the space. It looks guilty at being caught in such an awkward position.

I take the straight-backed wooden chair and try to still my quaking knees and thumping heart. What am I doing here anyway? I must be crazy, but, of course, why else does one go to a shrink? With that thought I giggle stupidly and wipe my sweaty palms on my good white dress.

The office girl comes in to tell me that the doctor will be in shortly. I hope she isn't looking at me too closely. The ugly blue finger prints on my neck are just about gone and my split swollen lip is almost unnoticeable under my make-up, but I turn my head away just in case.

The doctor shuffles in, takes the chair behind the sloppy desk, clears his throat, looks through some papers, clears his throat again and says, "What can I do for you?"

From somewhere a squeaky voice begins to utter hesitant, sputtering phrases. "Oh nothing really — I just want to talk. I'm fine — just a little upset — well, actually I came because — because — well you see, I have this problem." The words rush out, "I keep breaking into tears for no reason at all, I cry all the time." The voice fumbles on. Is that me and why does he look at me that way with a cross between a leer and contempt? Couldn't he say any more than "I see"? Oh God, he's telling me I'm suffering from a case of depression. He asks about my "ahem — sex life." I open my mouth to tell him sex is the least of my problems.

I want to tell him about the marks on my throat and my split lip and my drinking husband's rage. He silences me with a wave of his hand and invites me to climb up in the recliner. I get a gut feeling he's trying to seduce me. I jump up to leave. "Just a minute — take these three prescriptions and come back in two weeks."

I know wild horses couldn't get me back in that office. Head down to hide the tears in my eyes, I grab the prescriptions and escape. The waiting room is full of people. Maybe if I don't look at them, they won't see me. The walk to the front door is interminable. Steady, act natural — that's right, open the door, walk out, close it quietly so you won't attract attention.

Collapsed in the front seat of my car, I cry jerky wet sobs. For this I took ill-afforded hours from my job at the drug store? For this I tried for months to get up my courage? I might as well be dead, I tell myself for the hundredth time. I put the car in gear and slowly back out thinking about the night a week ago with the pills in my hand. "Coward! Gutless wonder. You can't do anything right. If you weren't such a flop of a wife, your husband wouldn't drink all the time. You're not much of a mother either, working all the time and dumping your kids on first one baby-sitter, then another."

As I pull into the driveway, I cynically remember my minister who tells me to be a good wife and pray a lot. "You two are one," he reminds me, "no matter what he does, he is still your husband.'' I think of my other doctor who keeps giving me tranquilizers when I try to explain that I'm coming apart at the seams, and who periodically sticks me in the hospital for unexplained viruses. I spit on a kleenex and wipe the black mascara from under my eyes, then I plaster a smile on my face and prepare to meet my kids and their baby-sitter. ''You're just going to have to go in there and try a little harder. Anyway you're too weak and gutless to do anything else.''

As I scrape enough food from the empty refrigerator to make supper, I think about the way Harold brags to his friends how I can cook a six course meal when there's nothing to cook. This cheers me up and while I'm cooking, I chatter brightly to my kids. Eight-year-old Brian tells me about his swimming lessons that morning and shows me where he scraped his knee when he was playing. Eric, two years old, hangs on my leg and sucks his thumb. His dirty face and saggy wet pants make him look like a little waif. Overcome with guilt and love, I curse the baby-sitter, clean up Eric and give them both a snack and a hug.

Seven o'clock, supper has been ready for an hour, the house looks cozy and the worn out furniture doesn't look so bad in the dim light.

Seven-thirty, the supper is beginning to look dried out and icky. The kids are clamoring to eat. I snap at them to wait for their father, then contritely set them up to the table and feed them. Eric has a runny nose and looks like he's feverish again so I hold him on my lap. Brian says grace and both of them stuff their shiny innocent little faces while I sit there and worry about Harold. I can't get food past the lump in my throat. I tell myself he's had an accident, something terrible has happened to him or he'd be here. He can't be drinking again! He promised he'd never do it again last week when I felt the sickening thud of his fist against my mouth and felt darkness descend over my head as his fingers curled snake-like tighter and tighter around my throat. I shake my head. ''Brian, mommy wants to hear all about your day.'' I know he is

slipping food under the table to the dog. Harold hates that, so
I let him do it.

I pick up all the plates but one and run warm soapy water
over them. Eric plays happily at my feet with all the pots and
pans out of the cupboard. I look at him with a heart bursting
with aching tiredness and love. I know Harold gets mad when
he sees Eric playing with the pots and pans but I think, "It
serves him right. He's not here to do anything about it."
Immediately I see Harold lying in a ditch somewhere, hurt,
bleeding; tears come to my eyes. I swoop up Eric, put away the
pots and pans and sit in the rocking chair hugging him to me
like a crutch.

After Brian and Eric stumble sleepily through their prayers,
Brian asks for his daddy. "You go to sleep now, Brian. Daddy
had to work late." Then I go look out the door to see if his
body is lying on the wet muddy sidewalk. Maybe he tried to get
home and couldn't make it all the way. He's not there.

I take a bath and brush my hair one hundred times. I
examine my neck — finger prints almost gone. I look at my lip
— still sore inside but looks pretty good on the outside. I look
critically in the mirror — shiny red hair, luminous blue eyes, a
roman nose with a hump in it (which I hate), freckles (which I
also hate), and a one hundred-twenty-five pound body flat on
both sides. I think of my handsome, muscular husband and
wonder what he sees in me.

Before I go to bed, I take one last look out the front door.
All I see is ugly blackness and rain; nothing is stirring at one
o'clock in the morning. As I shut the door not daring to lock
it, I wonder absently if a rapist will come in and kill me in my
sleep. "Probably be the best for everybody."

At three o'clock I wake up; still no Harold. Should I start
calling? Whom do I call? Not knowing whom, I don't call.
Back to bed just as the front door crashes open. Muttering,
swearing, crashes, bumps, Harold falls over trying to take off
his muddy shoes. The refrigerator door opens; more cussing,
more muttering. I lie in bed thinking, "Oh God, why couldn't

you let him be dead?'' Fearing retribution, I quickly change that to, "Oh God, thank you for letting him come home safe and sound.'' I can go to sleep now, three more hours and I have to get up for work.

It's too quiet out there; I can't sleep. Silently I slip out of bed. Chilled and goose-pimply I sneak down the hall. I needn't have been so quiet, his muscular body lies angled across the kitchen floor, one foot planted in the glob of mud in front of the doorway. I go closer, he snores, his handsome boyish face looks innocent and peaceful. He stinks. A feeling of helplessness washes over me as I alternately love him and hate him.

I hear Brian coming down the hall. Not wanting him to see his father in a heap in the middle of the kitchen floor, I scurry to where he is, "Come on, darling, let's go back to bed. Mommy didn't mean to wake you up." Lying beside him, tears coursing down my cheeks, I think two more hours and I have to get up.

I crawl into my own bed. It's no use to try to sleep now. I reach for my cigarettes; only one left. I smoke it slowly thinking it would serve Harold right if I die of lung cancer. Maybe I'll get lucky and get T.B.

Tiredness washes over my taut body, nerve ends sticking through my skin like straight pins glue me to the edge of the bed. Lying there I think about the past nine years and wonder why I believe him every time he promises that he won't do it again. At least this wasn't one of the times when he laid his work-stenched, whisky-stinking body over mine and tried to make slobbery love to "the best little wife in the whole world." Nor was it one of the times when he came in raging mad, flinging vile, evil accusations at "the biggest slut in town." This time he didn't stand me up against the wall and try to force me to admit that I had another lover and this time he didn't break up any chairs, throw any dishes or put his fist through the walls. Thinking of my minister I pray, "God help me to be a better wife and mother. Help me to keep my husband home."

Nine

As I sit in a chair, relaxing my tired body, I wonder how life can be so bad one minute, and so good the next. Tonight I really feel good. I paid off the last of two big bills that had been bugging the life out of me. No more calls at the store, no more threatening letters. It was tough to do, but I did it.

One good thing, Harold has been coming home after work every night for a month, and it is so great. He can be the nicest, sweetest guy when he is sober and we can really have a good time all by ourselves when he is in a good mood. Only one thing really bothers me about Harold other than his drinking and that is the way he treats Brian and Eric. He expects Brian to be absolutely perfect; he has never allowed him to be a little boy. And he is really hard on Eric. It's almost as if he is punishing them because I love them so much. When we do have a battle, it is often over them. But they love him and he tries.

I tell myself it's because of the difference in the way we were brought up, and who is to say I am right. I do wish he wouldn't be quite so quick to snap at Eric all the time. The charm he uses to captivate all his subjects captivates them as well and I guess they don't mind so why should I? I stretch lazily, better get up and get busy. Harold will be home pretty soon and it is time to get supper on. I hope Harold won't be upset because I spent all our money on bills. Sometimes he doesn't seem to know what it costs to live. He's really good at running up charge accounts and buying drinks for the crowd when we go out, and I shudder at the thought of a door-to-door salesman finding him home alone because he will fall hook, line and sinker every time. I grimace as I think of the day I took a lousy fifty-cents-an-hour job to help pay the bills, and on my very first day at work, a salesman came along and sold him a $300.00 movie camera. Oh, well, that was a long time ago.

Harold comes in, his face is downcast and resigned. He had to walk home. Our old car has given up the ghost. "What are we going to do, babe?"

"I don't know, Harold. I'm sure you can figure out something though." Once, just once, I would like Harold to do something by himself; make a decision without consulting me, or at least have some idea of what he should do, then we could talk it over. He eats supper quietly and goes right to bed. I'm determined that he should solve this problem by himself and I resolve not to do it for him. But the next day when he says he is not going to work because it's too far to walk, I call my mother and borrow her car for him to drive. He has to go to work. We will never get out from under our debts any other way.

Harold drives mother's car off and on for two weeks and ours sits. I hate him for that. Doesn't he have any pride, any gumption? I take mother's car back to her and tell her to keep it. If Harold can't figure out a way to fix ours, he can walk. Harold walks for about three days and his mother gives him a new car. It's a beauty, the nicest car we have ever had.

Life is great, new car free and clear, our two biggest bills out of the way, both of us working, and best of all, we are looking at a house to buy. It's almost my dream house, spacious and lovely with a big yard for the kids. We spend hours trying to

figure out how to swing this and planning what we will do if
we get it. I don't believe I can be so happy.

The deal is made and we are moving in. At last we will be
respectable citizens of our community. First we will rent it for
a year, and half of the rent will be the down payment. It's
going to be tough, but Harold is picking up odd jobs on
weekends and that helps a lot.

I walk through my new house, putting things away and
pinching myself to make sure it is not a dream. Everything is
so beautiful and spacious. Our furniture is pretty tacky, but we
can take care of that in time. The house is so big, our few
possessions don't come close to filling it, but we've decided to
make a list and buy one thing at a time with my wages.
Harold's been doing pretty good with his odd jobs. He still has
a night out with the boys occasionally, but mostly, he's too
tired to go very often. I think that is a bonus. I keep busy
dreaming, making plans and trying to do the best I can with
what we have. I am constantly pouring into Harold's ear the
things we need, the things I want, the plans I have for the
house. I'm surprised at me; houses and domesticity have never
been my thing. For the first time in my life I would like to quit
work and stay home with the boys. But I know I can't, at least
not right away.

When I tell Harold how I feel, he gets mad, but he confuses
me so much I don't know for sure what he is mad about. One
minute he says, "If you want to stay home, stay home. I am
man enough to support this family. We don't need your wages
anyway." The next minute he's ranting at me because we don't
have enough money the way it is, and he suggests I could find
a better job if I looked.

Everybody comes to see our house: my family, his family,
all our friends. They pat Harold on the back and rib him about
settling down, and ooh and ah over the room, the carpet, the
curtains, the yard.

One Sunday afternoon some of his beer drinking buddies
come out with a case of beer to celebrate. It is fun sitting out in

our own yard drinking beer until one of Harold's guzzling friends said, "Harold, you old son of a bitch, what did you ever do to deserve a life like this: a beautiful woman who is too good for you, and who works her head off so you can make a go of it?" The others chime in, "Yeah, you dumb bastard, you sure are lucky."

Harold laughs and agrees with them that his wife is one in a million; he would be nothing without me. But I know that I am going to pay dearly for those cracks; Harold makes me pay for everything anybody says and punishes me for every compliment. I wish they would never have come, I wish they would go away and leave us alone. I don't like his friends anyway; they are just a bunch of low class apes. I don't know why he can't see that.

When they leave Harold leaves with them. "I'll be back in time for supper, hon; we are just going to run over and take a look at a race car."

"Harold, why don't you take Brian with you. He would love to see the race car. Brian, why don't you go with Daddy."

Brian gets all excited and runs to get his shoes on and his hair combed. Harold walks out the door. Brian scoots out the door, "Goodbye, mommy. See you in a little while." I start throwing away beer cans and look out the kitchen window. Brian is standing out in the driveway alone, bereft and crying. His sturdy little body looks forlorn. I walk out to talk to him.

"Brian, what happened?"

"Daddy said I had to stay here and help you fix supper." He manfully tries to hide the tears in his eyes.

"It's o.k., darling, momma can use your help, but first let's do something you want to do. Want to play a game or something, or how would you like some ice cream?"

Inside I am raging at that selfish bastard. I always tell him that someday he is going to be sorry he doesn't have time for Brian, because someday Brian isn't going to have time for him. He never listens, just accuses me of wanting him to take Brian along so he can't go in a bar. "I don't need him for a

watch dog," he says. Harold always says he was never close to
his father and "Brian gets a hell-of-a-lot better treatment"
than Harold ever did.

It hurts me to see him ignore his boys so much of the time. I
don't understand why, if he was treated that way, he wouldn't
want better for our two beautiful sons; but I console myself
with the thought that when they get older, he will be more
willing to spend time with them, and he does love them. He
loves to show them off when people come to see us, and he
wants them to have everything. Everything but his time.

Harold does not come back for supper, nor is he back when
I finally go to bed at midnight. "Goddamn, that makes me
mad." We are doing so well, for the first time in our lives I can
see us being happy, well-adjusted, respectable.

I don't believe the sight that greets me on the couch when I
get up to get ready for work the next morning. Harold is (I
think it's Harold) blood from head to toe, his clothes are
ripped and shredded, his face is a swollen mass of ugly purple
jelly. Blood oozes out of a slip where his mouth is supposed to
be. Oh God, he looks terrible. How bad is he, his breath rattles
and wheezes. I'm worried and scared. "Don't let him be too
bad, God, don't let him die." He looks like he could.

"Harold, wake up, Harold. Are you all right? What happened? What did you do?" He gets up, goes to shower and
change clothes. When he comes out he looks pretty rough, but
I can see now that the blood is gone; he is not as bad as I
thought. On our way to work he spits out at me that three guys
beat him up in the bar last night. Three guys who are *my*
friends. (*My friends?* I have known them all my life, but they
are not *my* friends.)

"Good," I say as we pull up to where I work, "maybe that
will teach you to stay home where you belong."

It's been a strange week; Harold's been quiet and moody. I
know he is thinking about the beating he took. I have tried to
find out what it was all about. Harold's version is that they
just jumped on him for no reason at all. I can't be very

sympathetic to Harold, but privately I think if I ever run into those guys they will be sorry they ever did this. I am not above clobbering one of them with a beer bottle if the opportunity presents itself. I'm not scared of them either; I grew up with four brothers.

At least Harold's been home every night this week except when he is working. I giggle as I think that maybe I could get somebody to beat him up every time he goes on a binge. Wonder how long it would be before he quit entirely.

Ten

It's a warm summer Monday; hot already at 7:00 a.m. I had to walk two miles to work this morning. Harold hasn't been home since Saturday night. Why? Why does he do this when everything has been going so well? It's almost as if he can't stand prosperity. I don't understand.

The phone rings at the drug store; I answer it. Harold's boss tells me that Harold didn't show up for work this morning. "Oh, my gosh! I was supposed to call you and I got so busy, I forgot. Harold is sick today; that flu is really going around. I think he will probably be o.k. tomorrow though. I am really sorry I forgot to call." He is grumpy and not happy with Harold at all. I wonder where the hell Harold is and why he did this. One thing he has never done is not go to work.

I am too tired and too busy to think about it all day. When Harold doesn't show to pick me up from work I again walk the two miles home in spiked, pointy-toed shoes. Harold had better have a good explanation, that's all I can say!

As I painfully limp barefooted up the sidewalk, the landlady is coming down the steps, hands on hips. Oh-oh, I wonder, what is the problem now? I can't think of anything that would make her look so stormy. Whatever it is, I can't face it now.

Maybe I can stall her. "Hello, what a pleasant surprise. Come on in, we'll have a cup of coffee."

"No, thank you." Her face is red; she is really angry. In a voice raspy with anger, touched with embarrassment, she demands the rent that is two months behind.

"But Harold paid you; I gave him the money myself."

"No, he didn't, and I am not going to wait any longer. I have been real good to you folks, and you've got no reason to treat me like this."

"Of course not," I coo, "you've been wonderful to us, you're the greatest landlady anybody could ever have. As soon as Harold comes home I'll take care of it. Don't you worry."

"Look, dear," she says. She stops and shakes her head, "It's none of my business, but . . . oh, never mind. I guess you gotta live your own life. Just bring me the money as soon as you can."

I wonder what she means, what she is trying to say? The poor old lady goes muttering down the sidewalk, her yellowish gray hair pulled loose from a floppy pile on top of her head dangling down her neck like upside down question marks. "Harold, how could you treat this sweet old lady like that and what did you do with the money?"When he gets home I am going to tell him a thing or two. The race car! He probably invested in that damn race car! I'll kill him.

Tired and dejected, I open the door with what I think is my last ounce of strength. The phone is ringing; I grab it, stubbing my toe on the magazine rack. "Harold, hello, Harold." My toe is screaming, shooting darts of punishment up my foot. It isn't Harold. The manager of the grocery store informs me with a clipped, crisp, no-nonsense voice that Harold has some bad checks to be picked up. I tell him not to worry; I'll tell Harold as soon as he gets home. "I'm sure it was just an oversight."

I feel terrible, my toe throbs, my head hurts, my stomach rebels and behaves first like a teeter-totter, then a merry-go-round. Staring fixedly at the wall, my eyes fasten on a hole above the light switch where Harold stuck his fist one time.

"Harold, why are you doing this to me? I can't stand it; first the rent, then the bad checks, and where the hell are you anyway?"

It's dark, Brian and Eric are hungry. How long have I been sitting here? I feed them and we take my last fifty cents and walk down to the drive-in for ice cream cones. They are silent. I make a babbling attempt to cheer them up, but they sense something. Tonight I tuck them into bed with a story and when they go to sleep I lock the door. If Harold wants in here, he will have to knock. As I lay in bed tossing and turning, worms of worry oozing through my brain, I guiltily remember my mother-in-law's words about how a good wife always caters to her husband, having his meals hot when he is ready to eat, keeping the door open, being ready to make love at the drop of a hat. Once I tried to tell her that Harold was drinking a little too much and I suspected he had mental problems. She glared at me and said, "Men only stay home when they have something worth staying home for." I couldn't argue with her; Harold had borrowed plenty of money from her; many times she kept us from going hungry. I get up and unlock the door.

Pacing the floor, I alternate between white hot hatred and a sick haunting fear that something terrible has happened to Harold. It gets later and later and later. I'm on my second pot of coffee when the sun peeps through my kitchen window. "Where is he? Why doesn't he come home? If he is not dead, he is going to wish he was. Oh God, do something;" but he doesn't.

Three days go by. I tell my boss I have an emergency so he advances me enough money to pay the rent and pick up the checks. I tell myself I'm really stupid for picking up Harold's checks, but I know if I don't I'll suffer for it when he comes home, either by the humiliation of having him in jail or the abuse he will heap in great drifts around my person, or both. It's a lot less fearful to pick them up.

I walk to work every day and successfully manage to avoid my friends and family. I don't have any friends anyway. If

Harold doesn't chase them away, I do. I mean, who needs their sympathy or advice or the anguish in their eyes when they look at me. Not me!

Another day passes. I haven't slept or eaten since Harold left. I want to but I can't. I don't feel good, must have been drinking too much coffee. The next day I have a temperature of 104 degrees. I call my doctor; he advises me to check into the hospital. I don't tell him about Harold. I learned a long time ago that was futile; besides, it's too embarrassing. I check in, thinking this will teach Harold. He'll come home and his wife will be in the hospital. I call my brother, Stuart, and confess I don't know where Harold is. I ask him to keep my kids for a few days. He is coldly critical of Harold's behavior and says so.

"He's never done anything like this before. I'm sure something has happened to him. He doesn't have a thing with him, not even his shaving gear." I'm crying, so nothing more is said. When I get to the hospital I greedily accept all the sleeping pills, antibiotics, and tranquilizers. The last thing before I pass out, I call my husband's brother and tell him Harold's been missing for five days. He asks what I did to him and plainly doesn't believe me when I say, "Nothing." He thinks I'm a snob and that Harold married above his class. He teases Harold about being "pussy whipped." Harold idolizes him.

Eleven

The sheriff laughs when I try to put in a missing person report. "Aw, Harold's just out tying one on some place. Don't worry about him, he'll be back. What the hell did you do to him anyway? Must been somethin' or he wouldn't stay away this long." I slink out of his office hiding under a paper clip.

The minister prays with me for his safe return and says, "Whatever you have done to Harold, God will forgive you and so will Harold in time. You just go home and wait for him. He'll be back and everything will be all right." As he walks me to the door, hand on my shoulder, I feel as if I could crawl under it.

The welfare worker looks at me over her horn rimmed glasses. "Fill out these papers. I swear, you women that are always running in here. What did you do to him? Men don't just up and walk out on their wives for no reason. Are you running around on him? Have you looked for a job? Do you drink?" I walked out and left her stern, wrinkled mouth flap into thin air. The papers lay where she tossed them.

Two months have gone by and I know Harold is dead. I heard on the radio today that they found a body down in the south end of the state. I'm just waiting for someone to call and tell me it was Harold. Tears come to my eyes as I plan what I will wear to the funeral. I'll be so brave, I think, and I'll tell Brian and Eric what a good man their father was. My reveries are interrupted by a man from down the street. He comes in and says, "I hear your husband took off and left you like a striped ass ape. Is there anything I can do to help you?"

"Yes, you can get the hell out of this house. Harold is a better man than you are any day of the week. I don't need anything from you." Was that my voice? It sounded like it belonged to a mad woman. I went back to planning Harold's funeral.

"God," I say, "help me get through this, please."

The phone rings. It's one of Harold's friends. He tells me he owes Harold one hundred-eighty-six dollars and he'd like to bring it out. I'm suspicious of this, but as I start mentally figuring how far that will go on overdue rent, two months utilities and a bare cupboard, I know I have to believe him. This friend is an old school chum of Harold's. As far as I know, Harold hasn't had anything to do with him for a long time. Because, as Harold says, "The guy let his success go to his head." I know Harold is jealous of his friend who is doing so well. Is it charity? If it is, I can't take it. "No," I tell myself, "why would anybody want to give you anything anyway?" Better just believe him and let it go.

I agonize over all the bills that won't get paid. "God!" I rage, "What did I ever do to deserve this? Are you up there or not?"

The phone rings again. This time it's one of Harold's co-workers. He tells me that Harold sold him a motor and it's in our garage and he still owes Harold a hundred dollars. Can he pick it up tonight? I have the one hundred-eighty-six dollars, along with a few sympathetic looks and pats on the shoulder. I endure; I know he means well. But sympathy? Give me sympathy and I'll spit in your eye.

The guy comes after the motor; he brings a friend and they haul it out to the car. He hands me the money saying nothing, but running appreciative looks over my body. I feel naked. I run in the house and slam the door.

I'm still waiting for the call telling me that they've identified Harold's body.

Brian comes in from play and puts his arms around me. "I love you, Brian."

"Momma, where is my daddy? Do you think he will be back today? Momma, why did daddy leave? Momma, do you think daddy left because those guys beat him up?"

"Brian, I don't know where he is or when he is coming home. Your daddy is sick. You know how sometimes your tummy is upset; well, his head is all upset and sometimes he doesn't remember things. But he loves you and he would be here if he could."

Eric comes in. He's dragging one of Brian's toys. It comes apart, Brian clobbers him, Eric screams, tears running down his thin little face. "I'm gonna tell daddy on you," he sobs.

"Daddy?" Brian spits out, "Daddy doesn't even live here any more and he left because of you."

"Brian!" I slap him hard, he reels. He gives Eric one final shove, grabs his broken toy and storms out the door. Cradling Eric in my arms, I sob. "God, how could you do this to them? Where is he, why haven't I heard from him? Harold, you son of a bitch, you bastard, you dirty lousy piece of scum, where are you? We need you."

I settle Eric with his own toys and kiss him to soothe his hurt and go to find Brian. "Brian, I'm sorry I slapped you, but I need you to help me to take care of Eric. It's not his fault daddy left. Brian, please be nice to Eric. He's not very well and momma is really worried about him." My heart goes out to Brian as he bravely squares his little shoulders and his broad little body stiffens.

"It's o.k., momma." Arms around my neck, he comforts me.

It's time for supper. I go through the motions mechanically; macaroni again and milk. It's such a dull empty thing to fix a meal when no one is coming home to supper. The radio is on. The body has been identified and it's someone I never heard of. I'm relieved and angry at the same time. I can't stand this waiting and the dull, sickening ache, the emptiness and pain that make my movements lethargic and keep my head in an agonized stupor. I'm dying by inches. I'm going to lose my mind. "God, I hate you. Are you up there, are you listening to me? How dare you make me suffer like this. God, please don't let me suffer any longer; do something. I'm going to be the best mother I can, even if I am a failure as a wife. I'll show you, I'll show everybody."

The kids are bathed and in bed. I read to them, unable to hear my own words because of the miserable dull roar that lives in my head. I beg them to please just go to sleep knowing that both will moan and groan in their sleep and in the morning there will be two sopping wet beds.

Silence, alone, dark, pacing, thinking, raging, praying, damning, cursing, stomach full of bile and acid, head roaring, pain worming deep into my soul, threatening to make my bones explode. Early, just before dawn, I crawl into my sterile, empty, mocking bed. The hall light is on for comfort. I lay on my back, staring eyes glued to the shaft of light on the bedroom ceiling. My mind is merciless, I see Harold beaten, eyes swollen, ugly, body bent in pain; one of his eyes pops out of his head into my lap and stares at me accusingly. I scream and grab my head. "Stop it! Stop this now!" I must be calm, I must not give in. I must find the missing piece to this puzzle. I go over it again. The last time I saw Harold was on a Saturday night. He wanted to go out and party, but it was late, about 10:00, too late to get a baby-sitter; besides, my hair was in curlers. I'm a mess and I'm tired. He lies on the couch for a while and sleeps. His face is still bruised and puffy, but looks much better. I stand there and look at him. If I wake him up he'll get mad and probably stomp out. If I don't wake him up, he'll get mad and accuse me of trying to avoid having him in our bed. What to do? Take a bath and read a while, maybe he'll wake up by himself. He does, while I'm in the tub. He comes in and says he needs to go down to the bar and talk to a guy about some business.

"Why? Why can't it wait until tomorrow? Why do you need to talk to him at midnight?"

"Babe, why can't you ever understand anything? I have to see him tonight. He may not be around tomorrow. Honey, I want to talk to him about another job. We could be so much better off if I get it."

What's to say? Nothing! I bury my nose in my book and give him the silent treatment. Why does he ask my permission anyway? I hate it because I am naked and ugly and vulnerable in my tepid bathwater. He stands shifting his feet. I can hear the wheels turning in his head. "I'm going babe. I'll be back in an hour." He tries to kiss me and I turn my head so the kiss lands on a prickly, lumpy curler.

Maybe if I'd kissed him back, maybe if I'd gone with him, maybe if I'd said something he would have come back. I think how innocently I went to bed alone, glad for the chance to finish my book undisturbed, luxuriously stretching out in the middle of a sweet, clean, heavenly bed. The hour passes, then another, and another. I wake up to dawn filtering through my creamy lace curtains and reach out to touch Harold. Not there. I slip out of bed, look in the bathroom, the living room and the kitchen. Not there. Look out in the driveway for the car. No car. "Harold, you goddamned idiot, I hope somebody gave you another beating. Why, why, why do you keep doing this?"

All day Sunday I wait for him to come home, planning what I will say. One minute I am going to be sweet and sympathetic, the next minute I am going to scorch him with a red hot branding iron of the most searing words I can evoke to describe the loathing and frustration I feel. I am afraid to leave the house for fear he will come while I am gone and use it for an excuse to leave again. A friend comes to see me. I want her to leave and silently pray Harold won't walk in while she is there. Part of my mind is on what she is saying, part of it is preparing things to do if Harold walks in before she leaves.

I fix a large supper, thinking this sacrifice will contain the magic that will bring him home in time to eat it. When I crawl into bed with my book that night, I feel strangely peaceful. I know that Harold has to show up pretty soon. There is comfort in the knowledge that he has to go to work at 8 o'clock in the morning. One thing he has never done is miss work . . . back to the present. . . . I cling stubbornly to the thought that Harold would never walk out on his job of his own free will. He is too responsible for that. He's out there somewhere hurt, kidnapped, dead, sick, worried, alone. I wish fervently that I hadn't given him the silent treatment the last time I saw him.

The house shifts, the sound of a far off creak crashes into my consciousness; my backbone stiffens, my muscles are ridged. Fear jabs my body like stiff, frozen icicles. Breathing in ragged gasps, steeling my will to force my head to take over, I listen. . . . Is someone breaking in? Am I going to be raped, knifed, strangled? Can I get through this night? "Harold, you dirty, rotten, no good bastardly son of a bitch, I hope your soul burns in hell. I hope somebody pins you to the wall and pulls your fingernails out one by one and pours kerosene on your body." And then exhausted, humble pieces of my soul whimper, "Oh, Harold, wherever you are, whatever you're doing, please, please come home. I need you."

Twelve

Get up, go to work, laugh in the right places, cover-up, lie to save face, clean the house, cook the meals, smile brightly for Brian and Eric, ignore remarks, hear only what I need to hear, my mind must constantly work on the puzzle. Look for a reason, an answer, hope, pray, bargain, curse, take pills to sleep, take vitamins to keep well, read to escape. How can anybody be in such pain and live? Has it really been three months since Harold's been gone?

Harold's family doesn't come near me, nor speak when they see us. I know his brother hates me for the time I went to him and begged him to help me find a way to make Harold realize he was sick. I know his mother is refusing to see that he is gone, and is blaming me for the problems in his life. After all, she's done everything she can. She gives him money when he needs it, a place to stay if he's drunk, and she gave him a new car.

My family is nearby, but small comfort. Mom baby-sits for Eric and helps with Brian, but she will countenance no self-pity, no tears, no anger. My anguish is definitely my own. She wants no part of it. I feel her silent questioning accusations as she talks of only cheerful things and includes me in all the family plans. My dad, who hates Harold and never misses an opportunity to tell me so, calls him foul names and squeezes his hatred into every conversation. I want to scream at him, "Look who's talking! After all you put this family through with your temper and your drinking, don't you know I married him to get away from you and the constant sick bickering that goes on in this house?" I don't, but I lash out at him about his own shortcomings or give him the silent treatment with a superior look that I know he hates on my face.

All of my four brothers try, in their own way, to make time for me. They have their own families and pains and problems. My brother Ted, my childhood chum, my hero from the age of one, my protector and blackmailer, considers Harold a best friend. He is sweet and understanding, makes no judgments, asks no questions. I love him with blind devotion for this, even though I have never quite forgiven him for running off to join the service when we were kids, leaving me to fend for myself against dad.

My brother Mike acts a lot like dad, lecturing, dictating, making plans for me. He gives me a feeling of hopeless idiocy. Once we were closer than picture and frame, now distant, now polite. Why can't he understand that rejecting his ideas is not rejecting him? He doesn't live nearby; that helps. If he did he would hate me.

All of my brothers are handsome and masculine. They work hard, they play hard. All have been in sports, all have tried rodeo. The two younger ones are still rodeo buffs, very good at it too. All are tough, fair fighters. All have a reputation for being strong, resilient men. To me they are the personification of perfection and I wonder why I had to be the ugly duckling in this family. Once, I thought Harold was like them. Why, I think, can't he be like Stuart, my special, stoic, reliable brother?

I must have been about seven years old when I realized that Stuart was very special indeed. Finely chiseled features, blond silky hair. He doesn't look like the rest of us, with a handsome elegance that makes him truly my mother's child. He is as steady and sturdy as a concrete wall. He has driven me to work in a stony silence every morning since Harold left. He always seems to be the one that picks up the pieces. I try to tell him that Harold left because of something lacking in me and end by telling him to take care of his own errant life and mind his own business. When he is around I wait on him, hug him, feed him and tell him with my eyes I'm sorry. He talks little and seldom shows emotion.

Bernie, my youngest brother, is my object of worship. I idolize him, I mother him, I worry for him, pray for him, and share a closeness with him different from anything I have with anyone else. We talk a lot, about Harold, about Brian and Eric, about our folks, about his marriage, about my marriage, about the past, the future, the present, and our feelings. I can tell him things I can't tell anyone else. The conversation always ends with him pleading with me to think of myself, to be somebody. What a laugh! Me be somebody. I can't even keep my own husband home.

I have to move, I can't pay the rent on this big house all by myself and besides, I hate it. Somehow it's to blame for all of this misery I am in. Stuart helps me find a small place near my parents. He helps me pack and moves me in. My landlady is not sorry to see me go. She has dark, private thoughts about people like me. Brian cries "What if daddy comes home and we are gone?"

It's been four months. Stuart gives me a car to drive, and I find a new job in an office. It's a good job, pays well, and does a lot for my ego. Maybe I'm not such a loser after all. I make some new friends and tell them nothing about the sick, haunting feeling that is an everyday part of my existence.

I try to be both a mother and father to Brian and Eric, over-compensating for their pain and buying them things to substitute for their father. I'm beginning to go out once in awhile, and, when I do, I'm too noisy, too gay, too determined to have a good time. I drink and laugh, and flirt and dance and numb the pain with exhaustion. Harold's drinking buddies ask me out and intimate they are available for sex if needed. I lead them on and then chop off their heads. I am sick, flattered, disgusted and satisfied. Every night I both beg and curse God and Harold and every morning I wake up with part of me missing.

Brian starts school and I have a special new friend. Her name is Bev and I love her. Bev's husband is Bernie's old schoolmate who has turned into a hopeless alcoholic. Bev doesn't say much about it, but I think it must be terrible to be married to an alcoholic. I like him, even if he is always drunk. He's pleasant, polite, sweet and flattering.

I give up talking to God and Harold. What's the use? There isn't any God and Harold can't hear me. There is a strange kind of peace in blotting them both out of my life.

The pain of Harold's five-month absence has settled like a dull knife between my ribs. If I move carefully, it won't kill me.

Thirteen

Today I find out what everybody in town has known but me. Harold is living two hundred miles away with another woman. He is well and has a good job. My sister-in-law confesses that my stony-faced brother, Stuart, has known this since six days after he left.

The hot black rushing hatred I feel for this brother takes away my breath, as the agony, frustration and pain of the last few months wash over my body like angry waves crashing over the shore. I am going to throw up. I am going to have a heart attack. I am going to die, scream, pull out my hair, rip out my heart with my bare hands. I do nothing to give her any satisfaction. With a face devoid of feeling, I pour my sister-in-law another cup of coffee, light another cigarette and change the subject. While she talks, I think of ways to kill my brother.

When Stuart stops in that night, to play with Brian and Eric, the hatred melts into hopeless puddles of muck, as I think of how steady and good he is, the car he lets me drive, the food he brings and the silent love and concern he lavishes on all of us. I know he is hoping I will never see Harold again and he fears that I will go after him.

I do not tell him that I know. After Stuart leaves, Eric cries for his daddy; that makes Brian cry too. As I hold their sobbing little bodies, I vow that they will have their daddy back. Whatever is necessary to do I will do. He can't do this to them.

When Brian and Eric finally go to sleep I lay awake all night and plot my course. First I have to find out what he is thinking. If he wants a divorce, I won't give him one. If he doesn't want a divorce, I will threaten him with one. The next day I go out and buy a new outfit with the rent money. I go to the beauty parlor and get my hair done, and charge a stunning new coat; then I borrow enough money from Bev to fly to where I know Harold is. I do not find him.

When I get back home Eric is sick and must be put in the hospital. I sit by his bed for three days cursing God, Harold and a world that would let a little boy be sick without his daddy. I am feverish with determination. Eric will have his father. Harold and his whore will pay for this; I will be the victor.

When Bev asks, I tell her I found Harold and he begged me to let him come home. "I'm thinking it over, Bev. I'm not sure what I should do." I tell Brian that I know where his daddy is and he is well. Brian begs me to go get him. I do not tell him that I already tried. He cries and sobbingly, angrily calls us both names. He hates me and won't let me touch him. My determination increases. Harold will pay and pay and pay. He will be a good father if I have to give my whole life to this cause.

At least I know where he is, at least he is not dead, at least he has a job. But how, how could he let us go for all this time not knowing? How could he turn his back on us, shut us out of his life without a backward glance? How could he think he would get away with this? Why did he drag us down to this black private pit of hell? Why, why, why?

It's Saturday night. Stuart and his wife are taking me out on the town. It's to be a big time. We dress up and crack funny jokes and the mood is merry as we sit in the bar and banter. I

look up. Oh God! It's Harold — with her! Stuart grabs me and
gives me a lecture on pride, dignity, and self-respect. "If you
so much as look in his direction, I will never speak to you
again. Drink up, don't let him see you acting miserable."

My pride, my dignity, my self-respect and I sit there and get
foully, stinkingly, thoroughly soused. When we leave, Stuart
stops me from smashing the windshield of Harold's car with a
rock. I want to slash the tires, rip the car apart with my bare
hands, break Harold's neck. Stuart won't let me do any of
this. Instead he takes me home.

I go to bed, can't sleep. Agonizing, tormenting thoughts hit
again and again like bullets raining on a target. I pace the
floor, throw up, back to bed, get up, sit down, stare at the
wall. It doesn't make sense. Nothing makes sense. I'm a dead
person walking around in an ugly, steel shell. I find myself in
front of Harold's mother's house. I know she is not home.
Harold's car is there. I know he is in there with HER. Are they
sleeping in the same bed in his mother's house? A cold, icy
feeling is all around me. I drove over here, but I don't
remember it. As I stare at Harold's car, I see four flat tires.
Stuart! Driving home I swear to God that both of them will
suffer agonies of the damned before I get through with them.

Back home, I know it's all hot air falling in empty, useless,
meaningless threats. Nothing I can do to Harold will ever
make up for this damning, crippling, agony. With the crafty,
uncanny knowledge born of a sick, half-crazed mind, I know
Harold will never escape from me, just as I will never escape
from him. I know that if he ever stands still long enough to
look me in the eye, he will come when I crook my little finger.
I see with crystal clarity how she falls for the same charm, the
same lines, the same savior image of herself. I can't waste any
energy hating her. I need it all to get Harold back. I know time
is my ally, and I know just how I am going to use it.

Fourteen

Goal number one is to find out where Harold is working. Not too hard to do. Act like you already know something and information pops out from everybody. Send him a letter there with a picture of Brian and Eric, make it newsy and sweet, sign it "Love."

Goal number two is to see an attorney, file for divorce on grounds of desertion. Won't work; have to wait a whole year. Okay, use anything you want to, just file. No money, so no divorce, I am counting on that! Just give the lawyer enough money to serve the papers; that's all I need. Attorney is bored, uninformative, asks me little, tells me nothing. That's all right; he is just a pawn.

Goal number three, sit back and wait for Harold to come yelping at the impossible terms.

Goal number four — convince everyone that you really mean it. Who would believe otherwise?

I make arrangements to pay twenty dollars a month and swallow my guilt when my family is so obviously delighted. Bernie is happiest of all. Finally I have come to my senses, finally I see the light. I swallow the bile in my throat as he talks on and on. I want to tell him the truth but I can't. How can I make him understand that the one thing I want most in the whole world is to be free from Harold, but I am infinitely, inexplicably tied to him forever.

The "for better or for worse" phrase is branded into my brain "until death do us part." We two are one, and just because half of me does not know how to behave, that does not relinquish the other half from its obvious responsibilities. He couldn't begin to comprehend the single-mindedness of purpose with which I must retain my identity, must fulfill my purpose, must force the missing half to submission. The more I want to be free from Harold, the more urgency I feel to get him back before I commit the ultimate, most degrading act of all: that of giving up and admitting to utter, complete failure as a wife and a person.

Harold must grow up! I will make him grow up! If it takes every fiber of my being, that man will turn into a good Christian father his children can be proud of. I don't count, nobody counts, only Brian and Eric and they are second to my obligation to my other half.

As I knew he would, Harold comes screaming to the door one weekend demanding to know who I think I am filing for divorce. "You won't get away with this, babe, I'll fight you every step of the way. My kids are my kids; nobody else is ever going to have them. I'll kill the bastard that tries. You will never live with another man, because he won't live long enough; besides nobody could live with you anyway, you bitch, slut, whore . . . ."

When he's finished I invite him to visit Brian and Eric any time and sweetly suggest he should probably let me know before he comes next time. Stuart shows up at the right moment and Harold leaves shaking his head, muttering to himself. I know he is scared of Stuart. I despise this flaw in his manhood. Harold is stubborn. He won't be back for a long time, but he will be back.

Fifteen

My father is dying. We've known for three months that he had terminal cancer. He doesn't let up on me. When I am with him I want to say, "Daddy, I love you. I would cut off my head for you, walk barefoot through red hot coals, sleep on a bed of nails. I would do anything for your love, your approval, but I can't cut Harold out of my life. He is my life."

I'm crushed by the weight of his illness and my failure to ever win with him. Nothing I have ever done is good enough. Nothing I have ever been is good enough. He tries to talk to me about dying. I can't talk. He wants to talk to me about Harold. I won't talk. I escape from his presence every chance I get. I can't let him see what his dying is doing to me. I smile brightly and nod my head when he cuts me down, watching, waiting, dying myself. In our last moment alone together, I put my cheek down to his cheek, and say, "Daddy, I love you."

Chokingly he says, "It's too late." The iceberg that is me is seared with a red hot poker. A voice inside me says, "Okay, dammit, die. I won't miss you. I'll sit here on my ass and laugh." The grief I feel shakes me so deep it scares me. My body shakes in tearless spasms, arms and legs and stomach jerking like a senseless puppet. I go through the motions of being sympathetic mother, daughter, sister but I am laughing at myself. "Ha, ha, the joke's on you. He's gone and you're still here. He is done suffering and you're still hanging on." I don't understand this, I don't understand the grief. I don't understand anything.

I stand alone in the chapel. Daddy, the original love of my life. Daddy, the man who petted and pampered me when nobody else had time. Daddy, the man who told me when I was six years old that I was responsible for my four brothers when he and mamma were away. I remember it, like it was now. "But daddy, I'm not the oldest."

"No," he said, "but you're the girl. Now be daddy's good little girl and make sure everybody does what they are supposed to." I shudder with guilt when I think how I took the fly swatter and beat on all but the oldest (he could do no wrong in my eyes). Bernie wasn't born then.

"Oh, daddy," I cry, "I really loved you." I remember how he made my brothers give in to me on every point.

"Because she's a girl, because she's your sister."

Daddy, the man who never allowed me to wear shorts or a swimsuit even in the summer, but made me cover myself from head to toe. Daddy, the man who preached to me about pride. "Keep your face clean, your clothes neat, and family things in the family," he said over and over. Daddy, the man who came home drunk in the middle of the night, and waking me from a sound sleep, would cradle me in his arms and would rock back and forth on the edge of my bed, burying his face in my hair, telling me his hopes, his dreams, his love for me. Daddy, the man I wanted to protect from my mother's sharp tongue.

When did I begin to hate him? I think the first time was when we were going to a carnival and he teased me about being all dressed up and "pretty as a picture." "You'll knock 'em dead, honey. Bet you'll even find a boyfriend." Then when I did, he screamed, punishing me, castigating my mother for allowing it to happen.

When did I first notice that my tired over-worked little mother was a cast-iron saint? When did I realize that sometimes she and I were angels with unlimited talent, and other times we were too stupid to breathe? When was the first time somebody congratulated me for having my father's mettle and spunk? "She's just like you," they would say to him. My father would beam. When was the first time I knew that I would die before I'd be like him, and consciously decided to emulate my mother, even though I knew if I lived to be a hundred, I would never be as sweet and pure and beautiful as she? When did it dawn on me that the guys my brothers brought home were heartily welcomed until they took an interest in me and then they were "no good sons of bitches." When did he tell me that there were two kinds of women: my mother was the lady, and I was the unspeakable other.

I remember how cute he thought it was when at the age of five, I stood toe to toe with him and told him off. How disrespectful it was when at the age of twelve, I jumped between him and my brothers and took the strap on my own back, and how incorrigible it was when at the age of sixteen, I told him to go to hell.

I stand over his casket, sobbing, hands cupping his face, "Oh, daddy, why? What happened?" The funeral director leads me away.

Sixteen

Harold comes to see me to pay his respects. I listen to all his polite senseless phrases and go in the bathroom and throw up. I am cold, freezing cold; my body is shaking, I pile on sweaters and sit on the couch and watch him play with Brian and Eric. They beg him to stay for supper; he stays. Later we go for a beer and talk most of the night about the kids, the divorce, who will get what. I should get an Academy Award for my acting.

Harold asks if he can come back next weekend to see Brian and Eric. I tell him yes, and spend the next week cleaning my house, doing my hair, my nails, setting my trap. Before Harold gets there on Saturday, I go out in the street and pick up cigar butts and put them in the ash tray in the living room and the bedroom and the bathroom. I put on the most modest clothes I can find. Harold hates any sign of sexiness, or wantonness. I must be as pure as the Virgin Mary.

This time I only let Harold stay a couple of hours. I tell him I have a guest coming for supper. He is back the next day, and the next. As I cheerfully send him back to her and his job, my brain calculates — two weeks, one month at the most.

A letter arrives from Harold in two days, a phone call in three. He asks me for a date. I'm busy. He shows up anyway.

We go out. He invites me to come where he is the next weekend. I go and we spend Friday night laughing, dancing, drinking, reminiscing. Saturday night I sit at the motel waiting for him to show up; he doesn't so I call a cab to take me to the bus station and catch a 1:00 a.m. ride home. I don't feel much of anything on the ride back. I'm smug in the knowledge that soon it will be HER turn to sit and wonder where he is.

I am only home a few hours, the phone rings. "Babe? What are you doing there. Why did you leave me?"

"I had plans for today."

"I must talk to you."

"Harold, I can't talk to you anymore unless you are willing to do something positive about this situation."

"Dammit, don't use those fifty-cent words on me, and stop being so high and mighty." Resignation. "What do you want me to do?"

"I want you to go with me to a marriage counselor, and then maybe if it works out after a few months, we can talk about where we are."

I make the appointment in his city, I arrange for a sitter, I buy the bus ticket. I call Harold and tell him I am coming. I flirt with him, spar with him, seduce him, tease him and when he is weak with pleasure, I tell him he is coming home now, this minute or not at all.

On our way home, I hug myself, and sing to myself and think, "All right, my babies. I promised you your father, and I am about to deliver." I can't wait to see the delight on their little faces and hear the squeals of happiness I know will be there. I am not wrong. For the kids, it's like Christmas. They are ecstatic. I am smug, self-righteous, and everything is back where it belongs. Including Harold.

She calls, writes letters, begs, pleads, cusses, wishes us both in hell. Revenge is sweet as I tell her to get her own husband, this one is mine. "How do you like it, baby? Feels good, huh?" I give Harold a stern lecture on acting like a man and tell him he must tell her to quit before the kids find out. Brian and Eric must never know about her.

As soon as Harold moves in, he changes everything around to suit himself. The furniture is moved, the cupboards are changed, the decor is cut down and the rules Brian and Eric have been living by are changed. They can no longer do the things I have allowed them to do. They must toe the line. "Sit up straight, comb your hair, mind your manners. No, you can't do this. No, you can't do that." Sometimes I wonder why he doesn't just tell them to stop breathing, that way they could make no mistakes. Once, just once, I would like him to tell me I did a good job while he was gone. Once, just once, I would like to hear that he likes the apartment I picked out, that I have good taste, anything nice!

Harold is lucky, he finds a job in a matter of days. He puts in long hours and brings home a fairly good-sized paycheck. We try to keep going to the marriage counselor, but it's so far away and costs so much money. Besides, we don't tell her the truth when we get there. It's too embarrassing. Harold spins his lies, and I don't correct him. Might as well save our money.

Harold has been home for two weeks now. We sit up many nights and talk and I feel that I know him better than I ever have. He tells me all the things I did wrong before he left and I resolve to be a better wife. He promises to give up his drinking buddies and to never leave again. I feel close to him. I believe him, but I watch him like a hawk.

Where he goes, I go. When he drinks, I drink. Whatever he wants to do, we do. It begins to be a night after night affair. I go to work dead tired and hung over while he springs up full of life and vim and vigor. I keep it up for a month and I am sick with pneumonia. I refuse to go to the hospital; we can't afford it. Harold nurses me for three days. He wants to stay home from work but I won't let him. The money we are going to lose from my job is bad enough. I am really sick. I think I might die. I can hardly make it from the bedroom to the bathroom.

The fourth day Harold doesn't come home from work, or the fifth day. Brian and Eric have to fend for themselves. I call

Bev to come and help me. She is sweet and airy and full of life. I don't get to see much of her since Harold is back. Harold and Bev's husband hate each other. Each thinks the other is a rat.

Early in the morning of the sixth day, Eric and I are sitting in the rocking chair; it's almost dawn. He doesn't feel good either and I am trying to comfort him. I am heartsick that Harold would do this to me when he knows I'm sick. He promised he wouldn't do it any more, he swore things would be different this time. For three days now he has been coming home in time to change his clothes and go to work. I am too sick to argue and too weak and weary to care.

Harold comes in while I am rocking Eric. The minute he gets in the door he starts yelling obscenities at me. "Shush," I say, "I just got Eric to sleep. He's sick."

Harold reaches over, grabs Eric by one thin little arm and throws him across the room on the couch. I jump up to defend Eric and see a kitchen chair coming at me. I am screaming, "Who do you think you are? Get out of this house! Get out and don't ever come back! Why did you do that?"

Eric goes whimpering and limping to his room and Harold has me pinned against the wall with the kitchen chair. He looks wild. "You goddamn whore, sitting there trying to look so innocent. I know what you were doing while I was gone. You were screwing everybody in town. Who do the cigar butts belong to? Who did you go out with? You probably even did it in front of Brian and Eric. You're not kidding me, you slut. You think I don't know what you were doing? You think I don't know what you told everybody in town about me? You think I am so goddamn dumb that I can't see what you are? You're not fit to be my wife." On and on and on. Finally, tearfully, "But damn it, babe, I don't care what you are. I love you."

"Harold, I love you, only you, never, never have I ever had sex with anyone but you. You know that nobody could ever be as good as you. You know that you are the only man for me."

When Harold lets me go, I fix him breakfast. I put rat poison on his eggs. He passes out before he can eat them. I sit at the table, my head in my hands and I know for sure there isn't any God. I'm done, finished, helpless. He can do whatever he wants to do to me. I don't care any more. I don't even call his boss to tell him Harold isn't coming to work. From now on he can do what he pleases, but if he ever touches Eric again, I will bash his head in.

For the sake of the kids, the families, and everybody we know, I must be very careful to keep things on an even keel. Mechanically I go to work, mechanically I smile, mechanically I lie to my family. Now that I've decided Harold can do whatever he pleases, I give up. He stays home more and tries to be a better father to the kids. I don't want him to touch me though, and I am as responsive as a piece of wood to any of his overtures. Time after time we go out together and put on a front. Every time it ends with me assuring Harold that there is no one else. Sometimes I spend hours repeating the same thing over and over again, while he cries and begs me to tell him the "truth." I absolutely refuse to admit to something I did not do, even though at other times he tries to beat it out of me. It would be so easy just to say, "Okay, I did it, now leave me alone," but I won't. He is not going to win this one just to make himself feel less guilty.

I don't go to church. I avoid my friends and devote my life to Brian and Eric. I wait on Harold hand and foot and smile and lie to keep the peace.

The minister comes to see me. Why haven't I been in church lately? I give him a cup of coffee and some excuse, and tell him things haven't been too easy for me lately. I am embarrassed because the house is a pigpen. I don't try to keep it clean anymore. After he leaves, I give it a good cleaning. That must not happen again. That night Harold wrecks our car as he weaves his way home early in the morning. The patrolman brings him home. No charges. Harold is docile and charming. The next day I go borrow money to get the car fixed.

Seventeen

Harold wants to move away from here. Last Tuesday he showed up for work and didn't have a job. "I can't live here, babe. Everybody is against me. I worked my butt off for that guy and he lays me off, just like that, no warning, no nothing."

I don't bother to remind him that he only works when he feels like it or that showing up with a hangover all the time is not the way to win friends and influence people. What would be the use? As a matter of fact, I feel that maybe if we moved and Harold was away from his beer-drinking buddies things would improve.

I want to move to the town the marriage counselor lives in. I've got to give it one more shot, even though I know that she lives there.

Harold gets his old job back and we move with only the possessions we can get in the car, not knowing where we will live. The only house we can find is run down and unfurnished, but it's summer and warm. We sleep on the floor and live from payday to payday. Sometimes we go to bed hungry. But we always, every payday go out and party. I seldom want to go and never want to stay as late as he does, but I don't dare leave him alone. He might run into *her*.

Living in the same town with her really gets to me. Things I had never thought of before now pop into my head. I am tortured with thoughts like: How did he make love to her? Can she cook as well as I? Can I cook as well as she? What did he say to her? What did she say to him? Did he call her "babe?" My head spins with the whats and hows.

Every chance I get I dig Harold. I attack his manhood. I berate him for everything he does and everything he doesn't.

Every morning I get up and drive Harold to work and every night I pick him up. I have weekly appointments with the marriage counselor but Harold won't go. She has me in a group, but as I sit there and listen and sometimes talk, I get blind, dizzy headaches. Sometimes I can barely make it home. I can't let them know how bad I really am, and they mustn't ever find out how bad Harold really is or they will know I am not only bad, but stupid as well.

I am very angry; some women in the group are suggesting I am worse than Harold, and they point out ways I try to control him. They just don't understand. One of the women brings me a book on alcoholism. I glance at the title and throw it on the shelf. It has nothing to do with me. Harold could stop drinking if he wanted to. The marriage counselor gently suggests that perhaps I should think about divorce, but I stubbornly insist that Harold will change. He has to, or there is no way out for me because I am obligated to this death trap. That is it, that is all there is to it.

Because it takes so much energy to keep up with Harold, I haven't done anything about trying to find a job, but fall is coming and Brian is going to need school clothes and I am tired of having nothing. When the power company turns our electricity off for the second time, I decide that is enough of that and I go job hunting. I am hired the first place I go, and the second. I take the second job because it pays more. The first week I work, Harold wrecks our car again. This time he gets out and runs, leaving the car in the middle of the road.

When the highway patrolman comes to see if he is home, I suggest that maybe he would be doing Harold a favor if he put him in a jail for a few days. He looks at me as if I have two heads and I know he is thinking, "If I was married to her, I would drink too." He drops the charges and we drive around with a crumpled fender until his mother sends him the money to get it fixed.

Harold hasn't had a drink for six months, and I am beginning to trust him again. Together we go to the Salvation Army and buy used furniture. Together we reupholster it and shop for rugs and pillows to brighten up the house.

I have to force myself to forget about *her*. I don't drive him to work everyday any more, just when I need the car. One night I have to work overtime and when I get home the kids are home alone. They tell me some woman picked daddy up and I know it is *her*. He comes home drunk and in a sexy mood, "It wasn't her," he says, but a wife of one of his friends. Her husband asked her to come get him to help with something. As he forces me to make love to him, I show my disdain for his lie by lighting a cigarette, over his shoulder, right in the middle of his climax.

For some reason, everybody we know begins to come to see us. Family on both sides drop in for a day or two, Bev comes out with her kids. Bernie and his wife come to stay for a few days. It's a financial drain but I am happy to see them all, especially Bernie. He spends time with Brian and Eric and they love him as much as I do. Harold likes him a lot too. In fact, he likes all my family. Sometimes I wonder what he would do if he knew what they thought of him. Sometimes I wonder why they don't tell him.

The day Bernie leaves, I kiss him goodby and he says, "I am not going to waste any more time trying to get you to listen to me about Harold, but if you ever need me, you call me and I'll be there. But don't call unless you really mean it."

"Honey, don't worry about me. I am going to be all right. Harold is getting better all the time."

After he leaves I have to hurry. It is time to pick Harold up from work and I need to rush supper. Brian is in a school program tonight and he is all excited about it. I want everything to be perfect for him.

Harold is not at the place where I always pick him up. I wait for an hour. It's pretty cold and the snow is starting to blow. I hate to leave for fear he is working overtime and will come out and find me not there, but I am the only car there and it looks still and eerie. I have to go. Brian will be late for his program and we won't have time to eat before we go the way it is. I worry all through the program and I can see Brian is sick with disappointment because Harold is not there to watch him. When the program ends we drive once more out to where Harold works. It's really snowing now and roads are slippery. To cheer us all up we go to a cafe and eat and have hot fudge sundaes. Mine tastes like acid, and Brian and Eric eat it for me. I tell Brian over and over again how good he was in the program and he tries to be happy.

When they are tucked in bed for the night I read awhile and fall asleep. Sometime later I hear noises in the kitchen. The light is on. I stumble sleepily out to the kitchen in my shorty pajamas, eyes half open. I just have time to watch a glimpse of the room. It's fuzzy. There is blood everywhere; a man is sitting in the middle of the kitchen on a chair, a sheet is wrapped around him. It's turning red, three figures are near him. Somebody hollers, "Get her out of here!" Harold grabs my shoulders and pushes me roughly back to the bedroom banging my head on the door jam. "You stay in here and don't come out." I lie and strain my ears to hear them but they are whispering. When I wake up the next morning, the kitchen is shiny clean. Harold tells me I had a bad dream. I don't dare not believe him. But I am scared, I watch, and wait and go over the scene in my mind. Nothing happens. I never find out.

Eighteen

It's Sunday, Harold has gone somewhere before I even got out of bed this morning. Brian says, "He said he will be back in a little while." I put dinner in the oven, take my leisurely time getting dressed and feel good about not having to work today. Something is nagging at me but I am not going to let anything get me down today. The sun is shining and the house is cozy and it is a good old lazy day. The kids and I eat dinner and play a little game called I See Something (red, what is it?). We are laughing and having a good time when Harold walks in.

Harold is only in the house five minutes when our next door neighbor comes over to tell me I am wanted on the phone. Icy fear clutches my heart, only my mother has that phone number.

Stuart is asking me if I can come home; he isn't telling me why. "Yes, I can come home if you need me. What is the matter?"

"Bernie was killed today in a freak accident."

"I'll be there as fast as I can," I say and hang up. Back at our house I start to scream. I scream until my throat is raw. I can't tell Harold what is wrong. I can't talk, I can only scream. He slaps me hard. I still can't tell him, I can't say it out loud.

"Bernie is hurt, we have to go home."

I think I am in control but I get home with a suitcase full of junk. Nobody's clothes, only one sock, things like a roll of toilet paper, a magazine, everything that was sitting on the dresser. I don't believe Bernie is dead. He will show up any minute and everyone will hug him and kiss him and tell him what a dirty joke that was. Everyone at my home is in steely control. No one dares to let down his guard for a minute. One look at my mother tells me she is in real physical danger. I have to take charge. I feel that I have to see Bernie. I don't care what he looks like, I have to see him! They won't let me. The funeral home says no. I demand to see him but to no avail.

As I comfort my mother and try to help his wife to hold together, I am too heartsick to cry. There are no tears, only profound grief and agony and anger. I am very angry. Why, why, why Bernie, the light of all our lives, the one we all love the most, the one who has never done anyone any harm and never took, only gave? I cannot eat, I cannot sleep. I cannot accept this.

Bernie's wife, Bev, some of Bernie's friends and I sit up all night, every night, on my mother's front porch. It is useless and painful to try to go to bed. I am worried sick about what this will do to my mom, afraid she will never be able to get through it. Stuart is buried deep in his own private grief that he cannot share. He saw him die and I think he died too. Only his body is moving around. He and Bernie were closer than any two brothers could ever be, they were best friends.

Harold is never there. I hardly realize it, until all of a sudden I notice that I can never find him when I need him and I realize he is not helping with anything. How long has he been gone? I find him in the bar crying on first one shoulder and then another. He slobbers to all who will listen how much he loved Bernie. When he sees me, he attacks, "Don't you say nothing, babe. You don't understand what this is doing to me. So just don't say nothing."

"Harold, please come home, I have some relatives here that you have never met, and I need you to help me."

"You go home. I'll be there in a little while."

Absently I notice that the person he is sitting beside is a seventeen-year-old blonde who used to be our baby-sitter. I tell her hello and think nothing of it.

He comes home, but I have to go after him a second time and a third. Every time I turn around he is gone. I hope that our relatives don't notice this. Bev brings him home one time, consoling and cajoling and letting him cry all over her.

The funeral is over. Both Harold and I have to get back to work. We have been gone a week. I go out to the cemetery after it's all over and sit there by Bernie's grave until it's dark. How can I accept this? For the first time in months I pray. I pray for strength and survival, I pray for my mother and Stuart, I pray for Harold and Brian and Eric. I pray for peace, peace in my body, peace in my mind and *strength*. I go back to find Harold. I can't find him anywhere so I call Bev and tell her that I need a friend. All night I sit at her house and stare at the wall. She holds my hand, in silence.

In the morning I pack up the car and the kids and go to find Harold. When I find him in the bar, he is sitting in a booth with his arm around the blonde. When he sees me, he runs to the men's room. I wait for him to come out. When he does, he rushes past me out the front door. I follow, I can't find him. Finally I see him squatted down between two cars hiding. "Harold, we have to go home now. We both have to get back to work. The car is all packed; all you have to do is get in it."

"I am not going, babe. I called my boss and told him I was too upset to work. You didn't love your brother at all, did you? You bitch, you block of ice, you never loved anybody in your life."

"Harold, I'm going, are you coming or not?"

As I drive off and leave him, I see in the rearview mirror the blonde come out, and arm in arm they walk back into the bar.

Nineteen

The two-hundred-mile trip back gives me a lot of time to think. My anguish and grief is a deep, searing, soul-killing torment. Nothing I have ever felt can rival the despair. "Why Bernie, God, why? If you had to have somebody, why not me? Not Bernie, not Bernie." Bernie is like Brian to me. My mother bore him, my father named him, but from the time they brought him home he was indisputably mine. Mine to love, mine to feed, dress, protect. He slept in my bed and received the crooning, cooing, dressing and undressing formerly reserved for my dolls. One cry from him would send me running to his side; one yelp would send me bouncing like an enraged lioness to scratch out the eyes of whoever had dared to touch him. At twelve years old he confided his problems to me, at fifteen he borrowed my car and shared his first anguished case of puppy love. He was always around, full of kindness, love, arms full of presents.

Brian was his to tenderly carry and adore and later to take everywhere and tease. He was lovable, impetuous, full of life, always doing something for somebody. One time as a college kid he removed the back seat from his car and replaced it with a shetland pony, driving one hundred-eighty miles in the freezing cold with the window open, for the pony's head so he "could see the look on Brian's face when he woke up to a pony in the front yard."

Bernie, the football hero, the track star, the carnival king. Bernie the rodeo bull rider. How I worried about him when he tore up a highway to get to a rodeo on time. Bernie the army sergeant. How I prayed he wouldn't have to go to Vietnam. Bernie the humble, fierce, modest, competitive, innocent, daring, terror of the highways, angel of mercy, lover of life. "Oh, Bernie, I would gladly have died in your place."

The radio is playing a church service. I hear the minister say something about how God even takes care of the sparrows in the trees. Would he do any less for you? Angrily I snap it off. I am really angry. I am so angry I drive like a maniac and dare other cars to hit me. "This time, God, you have gone too far. You listen to me, I hate you. I hate you. How dare you take my brother? That's it, I don't care if I burn in hell. I am through trying to please you or anybody else. The whole damn world can go to hell. I have had it!"

From now on, I resolve I am going to live my life for Bernie. Guiltily I think of the way I just talked to God. Bernie wouldn't like it. There isn't any God anyway. What kind of God would let Bernie die? There is only one thing I can do for Bernie now. That is to do what he wanted me to do: to be somebody. "I'll do it, Bernie. I promise I will. I don't know how, but I'll do it." There are no tears left, just solid, unyielding resolution.

Twenty

As I go to work the next day, I only know one thing, I MUST NOT CRACK. I must not get sick. I must survive. From work I call my attorney, who was my pawn. I ask for the name of an attorney where I am. He gives me one. Without an appointment I walk in. He's a kindly old judge. He sees me too calm, too controlled. I have no tears, no feelings, I am a zombie. Looking him in the eye, I tell him I have no money, but it is imperative that I get a divorce. He must help me. I speak with such deadly conviction, he agrees. I don't care how he does it or what he says. I must do this for Bernie.

I am a dried up withering shell as I walk out of his office. The deep searing grief I feel for Bernie has turned me to stone.

Harold shows up late that night. I go into Eric's room and shut the door. I don't want to see him. I don't want to talk to him, so I write him a letter telling him it's over, all over. I leave the letter for him when I go to work the next morning. He is to be moved out by the time I get home. At work I go through all the right motions, but I know I must keep my body and my mind under tight control. I put an imaginary steel band around my head to keep it from exploding and force myself to eat so I won't get sick. Food tastes like straw; it takes a lot of milk to get it past the lump in my throat. I throw most of it up, again and again.

Harold is waiting for me when I get off work. He no longer has a job. Since I don't want him around, he is going to drive a truck. That will keep him on the road until I come to my senses.

Every night I talk to Bernie, renewing my vow to be something for him. Every night I suffer the death of a thousand arrows piercing my body, my hands and feet are shriveling, my stomach is a heavy iron ball threatening to break my spine. When I look in the mirror I see only skin and bones. Eyes like coal sunk into craters.

Six days after Bernie's funeral, I get to work at 7:00 a.m. and I'm told my mother is trying to reach me; call her at the hospital. She is there with Harold. He has wrecked his truck and is in critical condition. She has been sitting with him all night because his own mother wouldn't come. His own mother says she "can't stand to see him like that." I gather up the kids and go home, afraid I'll find him dead, afraid I will find him alive. As we drive into town, the truck Harold was driving is sitting at a station. It is the first thing we see. It is smashed flat. Brian screams, "Nobody could live through that. I know he's dead. I know my daddy is dead!"

In the hospital I sit by Harold's bed. His broken, bankrupt body swathed in a sheet evokes no emotion. His raw, black putrid oozing arms disgust me. I ask myself how could somebody like Bernie die in a simple little accident, and how could somebody like Harold live. The gray insensible, frigid steel that is me feeds him, holds his water glass, lights his cigarettes, mops his brow. I know where my responsibility, my duty, my obligation lies.

His family shows up briefly and are gone. They must get on with other things. I am hopelessly stuck with this broken shell. My family comes, one by one. I know they are asking the same question, "Why Bernie and not Harold?" My family must go to another town for an award service for Bernie. I cannot go.

It will disintegrate my person into a mass of slippery, slimy mucous substance which will flow through holes and cracks and I will be lost forever.

As Harold lies there day after day, the story of the wreck comes out. His co-driver in another room would be dead if it weren't for Harold's quick thinking. Though badly burned, bruised and broken, he was somehow able to pull his friend out of the wreckage, administer first aid, and flag down an oncoming car. I feel a grudging admiration for this superhuman act, and for his ability to lie there with a steely determination to make no noise, no fuss, no painful groans, no crying, no moaning. "God, this guy can stand a lot of torture." Why shouldn't he be able to, I think, after all he's lived with me all these years.

Staring out the window most of the time, I talk to Bernie, "It's going to take a little while longer, Bernie. I don't know what to do about this one. Am I maybe getting the wrong message from you? I have to take care of him, I am all he has. You do understand that, don't you?"

The blonde comes up to see him. She is carrying flowers and candy, arms outstretched, a pleading look on her face, stubborn determination in her movements. I say nothing, only stand up, my fingers grip the back of her neck with a death grasp; I guide her back to the door. Her mouth is moving, tears are flowing, face full of fear. The nurses stare bug-eyed as the candy and flowers go crashing after her. The vase hits her on the head, water is dripping down her back. A flower is stuck to her jacket. Harold pretends to be asleep.

The man Harold was driving the truck for does not come near us. He owes Harold two hundred dollars. I have to find him. I am completely penniless. When I find him, he tells me he is going to sue Harold and offers me fifty dollars as a gift, charity. I tear up the check and throw it in his face. I go back to Harold's room, call up the ambulance service and tell them sweetly that Harold's boss is going to pay for the ambulance to move him the two hundred miles back to a hospital near our home. They come the same day and Harold is transported out like a thief in the night. When Harold is settled in his new room, I go and find him a lawyer, who immediately bans all visitors. Fifteen minutes after the 'no visitors' sign goes up, two insurance men and an attorney come up. They do not get in.

Work. I must get back to work. How long since I've eaten, two days, three? Brian must get back to school. Eric, is Eric all right? The family who has kept my boys for the last two days assures me they are fine. It is night, the boys and I are home. I am panic-stricken, there is no food in the house, no gas in the car and the electricity has been turned off again. The sheriff comes by. Harold has bad checks all over the place. I only know two things: Brian and Eric must not suffer for this and I must get back to work. What do I do? Where do I go? Who will help me? The answer comes back, 'Nobody! Help yourself!" "Bernie, tell me what to do. I need your help. I know you're up there. I know you are watching me. Help me!"

I know what to do. I will go to the pawn shop and pawn my wedding rings. The fifteen dollars I get buys milk and cereal and gas for the car. We eat by candle light and sleep together to keep warm. In the morning on my way to work, I stop at the Methodist church. The minister is there; he turns out to be the one I knew when I was a little girl on another planet. As he listens to me talk about Bernie's death and Harold's accident, he is writing something. As I leave he hands me a gift of fifty dollars. "I can't take that. I will be all right. Okay, it's only a loan." Before I get to my job, I stop and have the electricity turned on. I takes every cent.

Twenty-one

The atmosphere at work is cold and unfriendly except for one co-worker who tries to be kind. Everybody has had to do extra work and put in extra hours because of my absence. They don't like it. The steel band around my head is all that is keeping me together. I watch myself work. I watch myself smile and wait on customers and answer the phone. Delicate as a spider web, stiff as a flag pole, brittle as dried flowers, I watch myself being very careful not to explode into vanishing powder. I adjust the steel band tighter and tighter.

Everyday I take Brian to school, Eric to the babysitter, go to work, being careful, very careful not to release any emotion or let the steel band slip. Every night I scrape up food for Brian and Eric, visit Harold, fall into bed, talk to Bernie with bitter, executing, circuit-breaking grief until exhaustion takes over. I trade my watch to the grocery store man for food, steal toilet paper and crackers from the place I work, smile for the kids, for Harold and for the public. Don't cry, don't give in, don't give up, and stop that shaking all the time. Somebody might suspect something.

My boss is concerned about me. He takes me to lunch to talk to me. "Could I use a loan? Do I need some help?" I can't talk to him then, I might break down. Can I come to his office after work? That afternoon his wife is cold and antagonistic, jumping on me, belittling me. I hear her tell him he has to fire me. I am a hardened, tempered chisel as I burst into his office, slam the door and demand to know if he wants me to quit.

The pain in his eyes is as deep as the contempt in hers. He says no. She says I'm not the only one who has lost a brother, or had a husband in an accident. She says she has no pity for anyone who would be married to a "no-good loser." He is flustered, telling her to keep quiet and me to come back to work tomorrow. I am speechless as I back out of his office. A co-worker tells me she is jealous of me. Of me? I want to laugh hysterically, but if I do the band will break and I will never stop.

Now, as a diversion, I play up to him, bring him his coffee, flatter him, compliment him, do extra work. She begins to show up the same time I do every day and is still there when I leave. I get a twisted feeling of amusement as she struggles to be nice. Without thought, without feeling, without mind, I stand beside myself and watch to be sure I do everything right.

My perfunctory visits to Harold give him no inkling of what I am going through. I hate him for lying smug in a nice clean bed, with people to wait on him and good food to eat. If I tell him, he will say, "You can handle it, tiger," and I will smother him with his own pillow. I don't even tell him I picked up all his bad checks. The bitterness with which I hate him is the glue holding my bones together.

Looking up at work one day, I see a well-dressed, dignified, middle-aged man watching me. I can feel his eyes on me as I take care of some other customers. When I am alone, he steps up to the counter and asks with a hearty voice, "Are you Mrs. M.? Can you take a break? I would like to talk to you for a minute. Mrs. M., I am from the welfare department. I understand you've had some bad luck." His voices crashes at me like a radio turned on high volume. I am sure everyone in the place can hear him. As he talks, I shrivel with embarrassment. I have one thing in mind, to get him out of here.

"You are wrong, I don't have any problems. Whoever sent you here is wrong. Now please, I have to get back to work."

The next day he is back again. Remembering his loud voice, I take him off to a far corner.

"Now Mrs. M., you have to listen to me. Welfare is not a crime. It's not a dirty word, and you are entitled to it. You pay taxes don't you? I happen to know that you can't live, feed two kids, and pay a baby-sitter on a dollar and fifty cents an hour. I also know that your electricity was shut off again yesterday."

My eyes are pleading with him, "Please, just get out of here and leave me alone," I say. "I am going to start working another job at night that will get us through."

"Mrs M., listen to me, you can't work two jobs; that is too much. I am going to make an appointment for you at the welfare office and you be there today after work."

At home that night, in the dark and cold of winter, I think about the appointment I didn't keep and the things he had to say. I don't know what I am going to do. "Bernie," I say, "that isn't the way to be somebody. I can't do it, I won't do it."

The kids and I play games and sing as we eat rice with sugar and water for supper.

The man, who no longer looks well-dressed and dignified but rather like a grinning, evil enemy, comes to my door. "Mrs. M., why didn't you keep your appointment today? I am going to make another one for you tomorrow." His eyes flickering in the light of my candle look weird.

"Okay, okay, I will be there," anything to get him out of here and leave me alone.

Again, I don't go. I don't have the gas, the time or the energy. Two days later when I leave work, he is leaning against my car. "Mrs. M., you are coming with me down to the welfare office right now or I am personally going to go to your house and remove your children to a foster home."

I see black, red, gushing rivers. I stagger against the car, waves of helplessness and fury wash over me. I have no voice, the band is squeezing, squeezing my head tighter and tighter. Mutely I crawl into his car, meekly I let him usher me into an office. A lady tries to talk to me. I can't answer. If I open my mouth, the band will break. She brings me coffee. She tells me to sign the papers. She will get the answers later. As I sign my name on the dotted line, one gushing, heart-rending moan escapes from my mouth. I clamp my hand over it tight and keep it there while she makes arrangements for me to get food stamps and has the light company turn the power on again. I feel like filth, scum, a maggot under a microscope as I spend some of the food stamps on my way home. In bed I say, "God, you won't even let me keep my dignity, will you?" Then I remind myself there is no God. "That's it, Bernie. It was the only thing I had left, and now it's gone. Now I have nothing left to give you, because there is nothing left of me."

The next morning my right arm won't work. It lies lifeless and still. I lift it when I dress and drive to work with my left hand. At work I cannot write. It's a dead weight hanging by my side. I call Harold's doctor. He tells me to come in. After his examination he says it's nerves.

I say, "All right, dammit. If it's nerves I'll make it work," and it does.

A friendly social worker comes by my home. She needs more information for welfare. She is sweet, pretty and young. I answer her questions lifelessly, wishing she would hurry up and leave. She puts a friendly hand out to me, I ignore it. With a rush of words she says, "I brought you some pamphlets on Al-anon. It's an organization for families of problem drinkers."

"You mean alcoholics!" I spit at her. "No, thank you, Harold is a lot of things but he's not an alcoholic."

As the door slams behind her, I wag my butt around in an imitation of her sexy walk and think what could she know? Young Miss High-and-Mighty. Everybody knows that alcoholics are soggy old men who sleep at the bar. Everybody knows that alcoholics are lazy good-for-nothing bums that stagger in the gutter and cry in their beer. Everybody knows that alcoholics drink all day every day. Harold is none of those things. He's just weak and spineless.

"Umph," I think, "just stay out of my life, lady. I have enough troubles."

Twenty-two

Harold can come home today. Three months he has been in the hospital. I don't want him in my house, but he has no where else to go. He will be unable to work for at least four more months. I know it is my obligation and duty to take care of him until that time, but I hate him. I hate him for the spot I am in. I hate him for living when Bernie died. I hate him for the loneliness I have, I hate him for the love and sympathy he gets from Brian and Eric. But most of all, I hate him because he is oblivious to the acid, bitter pain and anguish that has taken his place in my bed.

"Harold, you can stay with us only if you understand that I am going through with the divorce when you are well, and only if you promise to go back to the counselor, and only if you swear that you will be good to Brian and Eric. You are not to tell Brian about the divorce. He is hurt and confused enough. When you are gone, I will tell him."

Typical of Harold, he is as happy as a two-year-old. Charming and sweet and happy-go-lucky, he has no worries. Also typical of Harold, he changes everything around to suit himself and wriggles back into the middle of our lives. I swallow my hatred hourly and wait for the four months to be up. He still has one arm that needs to be soaked, dressed, and aired three times a day. As I am helping him, I can feel no compassion for his pain or the raw flesh dripping, draining, constantly manufacturing fluid.

I watch the wooden doll that runs this house. She eats, she sleeps, she walks, she talks, she has a too bright smile and a too shrill voice. She does not waste any of her precious energy on bitter words, lectures, or arguments. She is consumed with guilt, hatred, bitterness, grief.

Harold sees the compliance, the strange stillness, the lack of argument and lectures. Like a puppy, he wags his tail and tries to please, cleaning the house, cooking the meals, doing the laundry, spinning tales for the kids about their wonderful mother, how we met, what we did and making grandiose plans for our future. He invites people in for supper, dinner, weekends, and tells them how we are going to buy a ranch as soon as he is on his feet again, ignoring the fact that we are living from hand to mouth and the bill collectors are battering down the door. He does not keep his promise to see a counselor.

The wooden doll got a raise today and she feels almost human as she walks in the door after work. Supper is on the table and Harold gets a genuine smile for the nice, clean house and the warm smells wafting from the kitchen. A voice comes from the bedroom, "Mamma, come here please."

It's Eric, his voice sounds strange. When I walk in the bedroom, he leads me into the closet and drops his pants. He is bruised and beaten from the calves of his legs to the top of his shoulders. The steel band breaks! I flip out like a mad woman. I rush at Harold.

"You son of a bitch, you dirty, rotten, no-good bastard. You're not a man, you're an animal! Get out of this house! Get out! I hate you!"

Harold's hands go around my neck. He screams at Eric, "I told you not to tell, you little bastard! Now see what you've done! You'll be sorry!" He tries to smash my face with his fist and I sink four fingers into the wet oozing flesh that is his arm and I squeeze. Yelping and doubled with pain, he staggers. I grab Eric and head for the door to call the sheriff.

Brian comes rushing out of his room. Harold says, "Brian, come here. Brian, do you know what your bitch of a mother did? She filed for divorce. She is going to leave us all!" His voice spits at Brian as he grabs his hair. Brian is terrified, hurt, and crying. Harold looks at me menacingly and says, "Get away from that door. Get over in that chair and sit down or I am going to hurt him, babe. I will!"

When I move away from the door, he lets Brian go. "Brian," I say as calmly as I can, "please take Eric and go to your room."

Harold grabs me and sends me sprawling in the chair, towering over me shaking his fist, "I will leave, but I'll wait outside the door. If you try to go out of it, I'll kill you." A deadly calm comes over him, "As a matter of fact, why don't I do it right now, all three of you, why should I wait?"

Icy, inhuman fear rocks me; I know he means it. "Harold, darling, I'm sorry I hurt your arm." I must not show by word or glance how terrified I am. My brain is prompting, assisting, directing, restraining. "Darling, please let me get up and fix your arm. I know it must be hurting you. Darling, I don't care about Eric, I don't care about anybody but you." The nausea and revulsion I feel must be quickly overcome. Careful, stay calm, don't flinch, don't quail, move slowly, humbly, cautiously, warily. Your life depends on flattering conciliation and remorse.

Triumphantly he allows me to doctor his arm. Swallowing the vomit in my throat, I listen as he tells me there will be no divorce. He is the boss in this house, and I am a dead woman if I ever cross him again. My mind is frantically searching for ways to get out of this situation alive. I don't see any. I know our survival depends on my ability to be cunning and manipulative.

That night as I lie in bed, I pray and pray and pray for

strength, for skill, for patience, for relief. When I look at Harold snoring on his side of the bed, I see a fat, bald-headed stranger. When did he get so fat and ugly? When did he start to lose his hair? A deep feeling of peace comes over me as I watch him. I have no obligation to this stranger. This is not the man I vowed to love until death do us part. I am not doing anything *to* Brian and Eric by leaving this man. I am doing something *for* them. I marvel at the strength and peace I feel, and then as I stare at him, waves of overwhelming grief hit for my handsome, young lover who is gone forever, replaced by this sick, desperate stranger. With that knowledge comes peace and strength. I realize I don't hate him; I don't love him. He is only an obstacle to be dealt with.

In the morning I take Eric to a baby-sitter and call Harold's doctor. I tell him Harold is crazy, he must do something. He prescribes tranquilizers *for me!* I give them to Harold and tell him to take twice as many as I am supposed to. We live in controlled truce. Harold is at his charming best, complimenting me, waiting on me, rattling words of love and praise. I am peaceful, calm, and waiting. Waiting for the chance I know with certainty will come. My only confidant is Bernie.

Twenty-three

Friday, January 30, Harold has his last doctor's appointment. I leave work early so he can have the car. As I hum my way through preparations for supper, I feel excited and happy. Now he can find a job. At last the four months are over. Bev is coming for the weekend and I am anxious to see her. It's been a long time. My feelings for Harold have switched to the same compassion I would feel for any stranger alone and in need. I will do what I can to help him find his way alone.

Harold doesn't come back for supper, or for breakfast, or all the next day or the next. Bev and I have a good visit, marred only by the nagging worry that Harold will walk in drunk and abusive and spoil it all. Before she leaves I show her my divorce papers. She laughs and shows me her own. We both know it will be months before we can actually come up with the money to do it. As she is pulling out of the driveway on Sunday night, one of Harold's friends drives up. He tells me that he saw Harold the day before, drunk and happy and on the way to visit his mother. "I didn't know if I should tell you or not. I thought I would drive by and see if he was back yet. I know you're probably worried sick . . . ."

I thank him for his time and trouble and assure him that I

knew where Harold was all the time.

Monday, February 2 — it's snowing, ten below zero and windy. Harold is not back, I have no car, and no money for a cab. I have to get to work. I bundle up Eric and carry him to the baby-sitter six blocks away. Brian walks to school. Instead of going to work, I walk two miles to my attorney's office. When I get there, I am a solid block of ice, hands and face raw, feet numb and frostbitten. He's in, I'm in luck. He thaws me out with coffee and rubs my hands. Teeth chattering, I tell him Harold's gone, he's taken the car and what money we had and I don't know if he will be coming back.

He sits and looks at me and says nothing, visible signs of struggle on his face. He picks up the phone and makes a call. When he is finished he tells me to meet him at the courthouse at 11:00 with a witness. "A witness! That's impossible. I don't have any witness. No one in the whole world knows what's going on in that house besides Brian."

"Then bring Brian."

"I can't. Brian will never say a word against his father. I wouldn't even ask him to."

He is weary, out of patience, "Look, if I tell you that Brian will only have to answer two questions and I won't make him say anything bad, will that satisfy you?"

Back to the pawn shop go my rings. I need the money to take a taxi and pick up Brian at school and then to get back to the courthouse. In the courthouse while we wait for my attorney, I explain to Brian as well as I can what is going to happen. Brian doesn't want any part of it. "Brian, darling, listen to me. I know you love your father and I know he loves you, too, but, Brian, he is sick. If we stay with him he is only going to get sicker. Brian, he is a man who needs help, but we can't help him, we've tried. You have to understand that we cannot live with him anymore. He needs this time to himself to get well."

The attorney finally comes and tries to talk to Brian but Brian is sullen. He goes in to talk to the judge.

The courtroom is big, empty and cold. Brian is on the stand. My attorney's words are echoing, vibrating sounds. "Brian," he says with his arm around his shoulders, "did you ever see your father hit your mother?"

The yes is meek and muffled.

"Brian, did your daddy ever go off and stay away when you and your mom didn't know where he was at?"

"Yes," a little stronger.

Now it is my turn. I don't want to say anything that will hurt Brian. My attorney is careful. The judge says, "Divorce granted."

I don't believe my ears. "What?" I gasp.

"Divorce granted," he repeats. The courtroom is swimming, Brian has four eyes. My attorney guides me out of the room. I am giddy, exhilarated and FREE! *Thirteen years wiped out in twenty minutes.* I don't believe it. I throw my arms around my attorney's neck. He shakes me off, embarrassed and mutters something about having to pay for this himself. I'm wild with happiness. I want to tell him I love him, I want to get down on my hands and knees and express my undying gratitude for his compassion. Tears in my eyes, I look at him. Tears in his eyes, he rumples my hair and leaves.

The first thing I do before I even leave the courthouse is call Bev. She is dumfounded. Me too! Then I take Brian out to lunch. While we are eating, I suddenly get achingly, shakingly scared. Fear of Harold turns my limbs to jelly and my stomach to wet concrete. Where do I go to escape his wrath? Who will help me? What should I do? How can I hide? With an urgency born of fear for survival I know I must not panic. First pick up Eric, then go to the minister who helped you before. Throw yourself on his mercy.

At Eric's baby-sitter's house, her husband is packing to leave for my hometown on business. That's it! Stuart! Who else would protect me as well as he? Brian doesn't want to go. There is a party in school that day. Eric's baby-sitter says he can stay with her. Brian has been through enough so I agree.

At home, I throw the divorce papers on the dresser. My heart is pounding, my hands are shaking as I urgently grab a few things to take along. "God, don't let him walk in now. Let me get out of here, please." As we drive out of town, we see Harold on his way in.

Now that I am home safe with my mother and Stuart, I am elated. Patiently I explain what I have done. Over and over again I say, "I'm free, I'm free, I'm free," hardly daring to believe it.

Eric's baby-sitter calls. Harold showed up drunk, furious, out of control and took Brian. She couldn't stop him. "He told me you were never going to get away with this." I curse my stupidity and castigate myself for leaving Brian behind. Stuart and I go to the sheriff's house and tell him the story. The sheriff radios the highway patrol and we wait — and wait. I pace the floor and pray for Brian's safety. It occurs to me that fools such as I must be allowed to exist only out of God's infinite love for the blind, deaf, and dumb.

He's been spotted, obviously drunk and weaving. It's safer not to try to stop him though. The roads are icy, he might do something foolish. Every thirty minutes a radio report. He is being watched all the way. When he arrives, Stuart is waiting for him. Calmly he removes Brian from the car, calmly he tells Harold to go to his mother's house and come back in the morning. Calmly he checks all the windows in my mother's house to see if they are locked, and calmly he tells us to lock the doors and leaves. In the wee hours of the morning I notice he is sitting out there in the icy cold protecting us.

Twenty-four

Now what? What can I do? Where can I go? To stay in my mother's home would be disastrous for both of us. She is still reeling over Bernie. I can't give her any more grief. Besides, to go back where I started from is the final admission that I am a crippled, clinging, failure. I must think! "God, what is left for me? How can I live? What will I do?" Over and over I ask these questions. I know Harold will make good his threats to kill me if I don't tread very carefully. I must do the right thing, but what is it? The words from the radio program come back to me, "God even takes care of the sparrows in the trees. Would he do any less for you?"

I must get Brian back to school. He has missed four days already. In the safety of my mother's home, with Stuart sitting in the living room, I explain to Harold about the divorce. He knows, he saw the papers on the dresser. Even now as I look at this stranger I wonder at the wisdom of my decision and feel a fresh surge of grief for my handsome young lover who is dead to me. Harold doesn't believe he is actually divorced. He tells me it is impossible for it to be final until it is paid for. That is the key to my safety, as long as he thinks he is still married, he will leave me alone and continue on his merry round of work, booze, and women. I can go home in relative safety now and try to pick up the pieces. God only knows what I am going to do when I get there. I know my job is gone.

The house feels strange and empty. I give myself a stern lecture on not being afraid of the dark any more, many times I have been alone, many times scared to death, always knowing that sooner or later Harold will be back to protect me. Now it's me and me alone who must survive or die. The voices in my head are active again, "No, it isn't you, dummy. It's you and God and that is an unbeatable combination." Back come the words from the radio. I repeat them over and over, and suddenly I know I am going to win. Someday, somehow.

When I tell Eric that daddy isn't going to live with us anymore, just a visit from time to time, he says, "Oh boy, mom, is that a promise?" The dearest gift he's ever given to me and a phrase I would repeat to myself many times in the future.

Brian is hurting and quiet, suffering from a grown-up pain and guilt he doesn't understand. Harold has told him to take care of his mother and little brother, a task he tries viciously to undertake. I will spend hours, weeks, months, trying to de-program him from this and will hear from him over and over again the phrase, "But, mamma, daddy says he still loves you. Why can't he come back?"

I pace through the house, nothing to look forward to, nothing to do. The indescribable feelings of grief and failure follow me and engulf the room I am in. Finally I must do something or lose my mind. "Bernie, I know this isn't the way 'to be somebody,' but I don't know what else to do," I say as I go to see the man from the welfare office. "Bernie, I am sorry if I am failing you, but don't worry, I'll do the best I can."

Parked in front of the welfare office, I stare at the building, trying to force myself to go in. Finally I say, "God, I am helpless, a nothing, a nobody, take my life and do with it what you will. I give up!"

Sitting in the office, eyes on the floor, resigned and beaten, I think of my dad and his pride. "Are you watching me now, dad? Are you sick with disappointment or are you laughing at me?"

The man at the desk whose voice once boomed and crashed my skull, now seems jovial and kind. "If you could do anything in the world you wanted to do, what would it be?" he says.

The answer is meek but bitter, "Go to college."

"Well then," he says, "let's fix it so you can go."

Who, me? Realize a dream I have kept hidden for all these years, hidden so deep I don't even know where I pulled it out from? Again there are two of me, one watching cynically, unbelievingly, tauntingly, while the other goes through the motions necessary to make this miracle happen.

It's true, it's happening. My joy turns to fear, then terror. I want to cry. There are no tears. I struggle to cry, I need to cry, I can't. My stomach is a piece of lead, unyielding, unmeltable, unforgiving. Only my brain is engaged in this process. The rest of me moves at its bidding. My other self laughs, taunts, hurls insults and doubts. "Don't give in. She will go away. Keep your mind on Bernie, on your own goal."

Creeping meekly, struggling to be invisible, old as Methuselah, my ninety-six pound frame finds a seat in the very back of my very first class. The instructor comes in and begins to talk. Now I can relax. Now I can believe it. "Okay, Bernie," I say, "we are on our way."

"God," I say, "be with me; I am going to need you every step of the way."

Twenty-five

Where is the happiness, where is the peace, where is the joy that getting rid of Harold should have produced?

Life is a snow job, a contradiction, a farce. Endless days and interminable fear-filled nights, offset by freedom from bitter fights, drunken tirades, and unreasonable demands.

I am a sailboat cut loose from its mooring, drifting on a sunny open sea. I am a bird escaped from its cage flying blindly against a window, thudding against the glass until my beak is bloody, my wings are broken. I am a little league player safe in the outfield, I am a big league player caught in jeopardy between home and third. Run, run, go back, go back.

Being a divorcee is like wearing a big sign: COME ONE, COME ALL, MY BED IS EMPTY. Wives grab their husbands, like mothers pulling children from the path of an on-rushing car. Propositions flow like rain from a gutter spout, gossips cluck their tongues, shopkeepers cut off credit, and landlords give lectures on morality. Being a divorcee on welfare is tantamount to being a piece of dirty underwear left lying on the floor for everyone to see.

Bev has moved nearby and is enrolled in college, too. Even though we don't take the same classes, I know I couldn't make it if it weren't for her. I have never felt more lonely, more bereft, more of a failure. I have never felt more guilty, more mortified, or more degraded. Bev and I cling together like the last two survivors on a ship overtaken by plague. Like chickens who have lost their feathers, we painfully struggle to cover our nakedness.

I have no blood in my veins, only the thick, brown muddy water of bitterness, and the murky, churning masses of self-hatred. The thick gray mask of clay I have worn for so long has hardened into steel armor, allowing nothing to penetrate. Except for fear and terror I am emotionally drained. I cannot laugh, I cannot cry, I cannot feel. My every act is a put-on: nod your head when others speak, laugh when others laugh, go through the motions of living, always careful, always controlled. There is a whole new set of rules to live by and I don't know what they are.

Where is the woman with the spunk, the ability to survive? Where is the Mother Confident? Where is the person who could spit in your eye at the least provocation? Is she gone, lost forever like snow on a sunny day? She is fading fast and taking her place is an impotent worm squirming deeper and deeper into earthy rocky soil.

Brian and Eric and I have moments of simple uncomplicatedness in our lives, but always in the back of my mind is fear. I never go anywhere without them or let them go anywhere without me. They cannot pass the boundaries of their front yard but I watch them from the window. Harold must never be in a position to grab them and run. There is always the possibility that he might show up, and he does, sometimes drunk, sometimes sober, but always crying, pleading, begging, "You've got to come back, I need you. Don't you understand, babe, I gotta have you to lean on."

Wearily I say, "Harold, I can't hold you up any longer."

It is 2:00 a.m. The phone beside my bed rings. Groggily I fumble for it, "Uh, hello." It's Harold, again cursing, screaming drunkenly, slurring his words. I listen mesmerized to the evil flowing from the receiver, like a hypnotized bug under a heel. Finally I say, "Harold, I need some time, I have to be by myself for a while. My head is all messed up." Could that be true? No, it's his head that is messed up, not mine, the only thing wrong with me is him.

I am back home for a holiday, sitting in a bar with friends. Harold walks up, sinks to his knees, hands clasped in a praying position, "I'm begging you, babe. Is this what you want?" My friends are embarrassed. "Please, you have to talk to me. I am not leaving here until you do."

"Go with him," they say.

I resist. "Heartless tramp," their eyes are saying. "How could you be so cruel?"

I go. When I come back, my nose is broken, my clothes ripped to shreds, my body a punching bag. All in the name of love.

I come home from school. Harold is in my house; he has gone through every nook, every cranny, every drawer. In his hands are a stack of letters from Pete. "How long have you been writing to Pete?"

"What difference does it make? It doesn't mean anything."

Grabbing my shoulder he shoves the letters in my face, "Doesn't mean anything, the son of a bitch is in love with you. Read this. Read these."

"Harold, I have read them." Do I ask him what he is doing in my house? No. Do I ask why he is going through my mail? No. "Harold," I say, "why don't you go play with the kids while I fix supper."

He comes, he goes, he begs, he threatens, he cries, he curses, he destroys my car, he threatens suicide, HE DRINKS. I am beginning to wonder if there is something to the theory that he could be an alcoholic, but what does that mean? I am still hopelessly trapped. I still believe that whatever he is, it is all my fault. When he is at his nicest, most charming best, I look at him and think, no, Harold is not an alcoholic. Alcoholics are not nice, they are full time drunks with bulbous red noses.

Pete writes that he has been transferred to England. He will buy the tickets if I will come over. I decide to go. He wants to marry me. Why not? I know that I have to get away from Harold. I am beginning to see that I have a sick need for Harold's attention, but why? Late at night, alone with my thoughts, I say, "Bernie, I need Harold like an alcoholic needs a drink." Over and over I fight the urge to say, "Okay, I give, come on back."

I decide that before I give Pete an answer I will investigate this Al-anon thing I have heard about. Maybe I won't go. Maybe I will just find out when it is. I am too embarrassed to ask anyone, so I write to the social worker telling her it is for a friend. I find out, but when the night comes I can't go. I don't have the nerve. "You gutless wonder," I say to myself in the mirror, "you are hopelessly dumb, stupid, and incompetent."

"No, I'm not," I say, "I'll go to England and I'll marry Pete."

School is out for the summer and wonder of wonders, my grades are good.

My mother says, "Don't go." My welfare worker says, "I will give you sixty days to change your mind."

Bev acts like I am deserting the ship.

In England Pete is sweet, attentive, gentle, and humble. He spoils Brian and dotes on Eric. Together we do all the touristy things and I am euphoric for the first few days, but it begins to be a strain, something is wrong. I try to convince myself that Pete is the answer to my prayers, but it's no good. Over here, away from the pressure, I know I need more help than Pete can give me. With a great deal of surprise I discover I can't escape from the biggest problem — me. "God, let me explain it to him so he will understand." Gently I try to tell Pete that I would be doing a terrible thing to him if I were to marry him now. He is very angry. I am pleading with him to understand. "Pete, please send me back, I'm sick." I didn't mean to say that, why did I say that? Pete doesn't understand, neither do I.

On the last day of my sixty days, I walk into my welfare worker's office. I am ready to go back to school, my desire for knowledge is stronger than my fear. He is delighted and shakes my hand, pumping my arm, patting my shoulder.

Twenty-six

Slinking around the campus, head down, I scurry from class to class, speaking to no one. Crushed by the sheer weight of daring to be there, I can barely function. Only in class can I relax. There I am avid for knowledge, trying to inhale academia. These are my good days; on bad days I can't force myself out my front door. It is when the bad days outnumber the good two to one that I have to do something. I am going to find that Al-anon group and this time I am going to go. Harold may not be an alcoholic, but at least there will be real, live people who can tell me what one is.

This must be the way a pilot feels in the last seconds before he is going to crash. In a cold sweat, hands shaking, knees knocking, filled with sheer terror, I push open the door that will lead me to the meeting. What will they think of me? Will they be smug and self-righteous or will they understand? "Oh, please understand," I breathe as I find a chair. A woman smiles at me, I give her a tentative non-committal grimace that I hope passes for a smile. I am surprised there are only a few women there. I'd expected more. One woman has a purplish black eye and a swollen face. Instinctively I know how she got it. At least I am not the only one, I think. They take turns talking and I am confused. Some things sound like Harold and some don't. I leave with a sick, pounding headache. At home I decide they are all a bunch of crazies and I have enough troubles without listening to theirs. The next minute I think maybe they know something I don't. They seem so calm and so accepting. "Well, they're all nuts," I say as I pull the covers over my head. Still when the time comes, I go back again, and again. I listen but I don't talk unless spoken to, and then only to protest my innocence. Habitually I rush home after each meeting and gulp down aspirin for my screaming head.

One day scurrying across the campus I pass Elaine. She is from the group. I am surprised. I didn't know she was in school, too. "Well, misfit," I think, "if you didn't always have your head down, you might see something." I want to speak but instead I avert my eyes. What if she doesn't remember me?

Elaine is tall, cool, and competent. "Tonight," she says, "how about going somewhere for a while after the meeting and we can talk." I am so grateful for her attention, I practically wag my tail. We discuss our children. She has four. I tell her a little about Harold, making sure she knows what a bastard he is.

As I get farther and farther into this new year of school, I am hurt by the growing distance between Bev and me. Bev is busy and involved, seldom having time for me. We still call each other for emergencies but the old closeness is gone. I realize with pain that we both have to grow in our own way, and I fall back on one of the Al-anon phrases, "Live and Let Live." Still, it's difficult.

I realize that without even trying, I am beginning to use that phrase and others for comfort and strength.

I have a lot of trouble with some of the Al-anon concepts, particularly the idea that anyone who has problems caused by someone else's drinking is a co-alcoholic. They can say what they like, I refuse to be a co-alcoholic.

Al-anon talks a lot about detachment. I have struggled and

struggled with that word. In my mind, the difference between being detached and being a doormat is not clearly defined. The same people who talk about being detached are obviously very attached. At what point do I cease being detached and start being a doormat? Will I ever see the day I will be confident of my own ability to think for myself? In what instances do I mind my own business and in what instances do I take action? It is all too deep for me, I don't even begin to understand where one gets the technique of not being personally involved when one is personally involved.

Twenty-seven

Harold comes around less and less, and the boys and I have our routine down pat. There is no money for extras, and if anyone needs luxuries like medicine or shoes, we are in deep trouble. A feeling of closeness exists in our house. At least we are all in the same corner, although Brian is at times deeply troubled. I have a copy of the serenity prayer hanging over my sink in the kitchen, and I study it a lot, reading it out loud as I do the dishes: "God, grant me the serenity to accept the things I cannot change, the courage to change the things I can, and the wisdom to know the difference." But still there are those crippling, aching moments of loneliness and terror at night.

Elaine is having coffee in my kitchen. The seepage of my bitterness is still flowing, sour, and pungent. She pulls no punches. Looking me in the eye she says, "You like being persecuted, you love being 'poor little me.' How much of your life are you going to spend whining away? For God's sake, he's gone. Let him go!" Now is that fair after all I have been through? She doesn't understand, but I know that she does. If anything, her life has been worse than mine. Later she apologizes saying, "He is a grown man. Do you think you are God that you can make people drink or not drink? Did you put it in his hand and lift it to his mouth?''

Elaine and I go downtown for a while and the sheer luxury of being able to come and go at will leaves me breathless.

At the next meeting of the group, I feel as if I am in the middle of a conspiracy as the attention seems to focus on me. "Reach out," they say, "you are so contained, so remote, you're so distant."

I want to shout at them, "Don't you think I know that, don't you think I want to feel happiness, don't you think I want to jump up and down, and don't you think I want to cry when I'm sad, and don't you know I can't?" I am a robot disguised as a person and each step I take, each move I make must be programmed like a computer.

"Try," they say, "try just smiling at people and saying hello instead of acting like they are invisible."

"But it's not them that's invisible, it's me!" But they say, "They don't know that." "What if nobody smiles back, what if I really am invisible?"

"You aren't," they say.

Later Elaine says, "That's a beautiful sweater you're wearing tonight." I mumble something about it being old and ugly. She says, "Are you saying I don't have any taste?"

Surprised, I say no.

"Are you saying I don't know a beautiful sweater when I see one?"

"No."

"Well, then just say thank you."

Meekly I say, "Thank you, Elaine."

I am determined I am going to walk instead of scurry, head up instead of down. Forcing myself to go slowly, I meet two girls on the walk. One smiles and says, "Hello." I meet her eyes but say nothing. "Stuck up old bag," she mutters. The rest of the day, I smile at everybody that comes near. The 'hello' gets stuck in my throat sometimes and the end of the day finds me exhausted with the effort and feeling like a grinning idiot. In history class some days later I hesitantly suggest to the woman sitting beside me that maybe we could have coffee after class. She accepts gratefully and later tells me how lonesome she has been being older than everyone else in school.

"Oh, hey, I know the feeling." Why did I never notice her before? Sue is also divorced and still reeling from the blow of waking up to discover her husband had sold the house and furniture right out from under her and their child.

Carried along on the coat tails of Sue and Elaine, I begin to meet people, usually ending up cursing myself and my stupidity for saying either nothing or the wrong thing.

I haunt the book stores in my spare time, looking for books that will tell me who I am. My bedside stand is covered with 'how to' books. How to like yourself, assert yourself, understand yourself, live with yourself, self, self, self. I avidly read them, every one, often making notes and writing out pertinent phrases and quotations. Still I find that only anger has the power to move me from one place to another.

"Help, somebody help. Please, help me." I am down in a hole, the walls are high and slippery. Again and again I tackle the wall, reaching, struggling, slipping. My hands and feet and knees are bloody, making ugly stains on the black, slimy sides. Harold peers over the side and grins an evil grin and drops a rope half-way down. A woman circles the hole throwing stones, laughing and jeering as I duck and bob to miss being hit.

It's that dream again, Sweaty and shaken I wake, struggling to consciousness, wild eyes darting around the dimly lit room. I look at my hands, no blood. "What does it mean?" I ask myself as I slip from my warm treacherous bed and go to make sure Brian and Eric are safely asleep in the next room. For the hundredth time I ask myself what they are going through, stuck with a drunken father and a crippled, insipid mother. What ever it is, I tell myself that it's better than they had before. At least they can go off to school without the ringing of bitter fights in their ears. At least no one asks them to be perfect. At least they only have one person telling them what to do rather than the conflicting orders they formerly received. But still I wonder, the sadness in Brian's eyes haunts me. Eric seems to be the only one profiting by all this. He will never again experience the pain of physical abuse, but what is happening to his head?

My first date. I don't want to go. I do want to go. I'm scared. What will I say? How will I act? I think of my surprise and how I stuttered when he actually asked me for a date. Not that I didn't set him up. In a cool, calculated way, feeling no guilt or even much attraction I tested my powers. He is here. The urge to lock myself in my bedroom is strong, but the baby-sitter is present and I don't want to look foolish. Shy and unsure, like a thirteen-year-old on her first date, I am nevertheless cool, remote, impeccably dressed, every hair in place. I say what I think he wants to hear and am rewarded by hearing the response I thought I would get. When you are invisible, you can be anyone you choose.

One date leads to another, and I win other male friends. No one I particularly care for, each one another experiment in power, until I meet Bill, and I am wary of him. He stops by my house constantly. When I open the door and he is there, I want to slam it in his face, but I don't.

One day Bill is on his way out, kissing me goodbye, as Brian walks in. With a stricken look, Brian marches resolutely to his room, slamming the door. Sounds of rage ensue. Thud, thump, I hear. Crash! Bang! Things hit the wall.

"Brian, please come out and eat with us. Eric and I don't want to eat supper alone."

"I'm not hungry."

"Then just come out and sit with us, please."

An eleven year old body, contorted in red-faced fury pops out from behind the door. "Why? Why should I?"

"Because I love you."

Fury dissolves into tears. At the table, "Mom, what would you do if I ran away?"

"I'd call out the national guard and scour the countryside until I found you."

"And then what, tie me up or beat me?"

"Nope; smother you with kisses and tickle you until you die laughing."

"Oh, mom, that's dumb."

"So is running away."

"I know."

Twenty-eight

I sit quietly waiting for the rest of Al-anon group to show up. I don't know why I came. My head is the playground of a boomerang. With my fingers gently pressed to my temples, I feel it — boom-er-rang, boom-er-rang, boom-er-rang. My mouth feels like it was open when the birds flew over and my jellyfish stomach is oozing danger signals. Miserably I sit and listen as the meeting opens and others are talking. The leader looks at me, "Anything you want to share?"

"No," I say, "I don't feel like talking. I'm tired and I have a massive hangover." That does it, I think, as everybody swivels to stare. Now I will be kicked out. Well, who the hell cares, I won't wait for them to tell me, I'll leave. I stand up but people are surging around me hugging me, kissing me. Why, because I have a hangover? The tears start to flow; once started, they cannot be cut off.

Agonized sobs coming from a distance, anguish in a disparaged voice, it's me. Arms are still holding me tight, "That's right, let it out, go ahead and cry."

Live, warm, caring, human people are listening as I spew out the venomous garbage from my gut. It dawns on me that these are women and I have never liked women, except one or two here and there. Women are petty, empty-headed; they are sewer cats, stewing around in the mulch of their servitude. At the edge of my brain multitudes of thoughts strike like lightning outside a window. I can almost hear the crash of thunder as things begin to fall in place and words begin to penetrate the fog of my tears.

"I love you," I hear, and the voice is so warm, so caressing it brings fresh spasms of warm, cleansing, salty tears. All the Al-anon slogans I have been hearing these many months, all the self-improvement books I have read, all the psychology courses in the last two and a half years, are beginning to take vague, shifting shape. Sobbing, I blubber out the words, "I need your help, I'm sick, I'm a co-alcoholic."

One member smilingly accepts my admission and says, "We kind of suspected you were coming here for a reason." Like a magnet picking up pins through open pores, I am feeling. I am feeling! The impervious lump of lead that has been resolutely lodged in my stomach is vanished, gone, and I am floating on air.

Riding home with Elaine, I say, "How could I be so blind for so long?"

Patting me on the shoulder, she says simply, "We have all been there." The simplicity of it all, the magnitude it encompasses!

Gliding through my house, two feet off the floor, humming through preparations for bed, I am simultaneously ecstatic and humble. Eric moans in his sleep, I slip to his side, rubbing his back. Brian lies sleeping in sweet innocence. My love for them permeates the air, surely it must penetrate their very bones. Oh, Eric darling. Oh, Brian sweetheart, if only I could share with you the things I have learned tonight. "Oh, God in heaven, thank you. Thank you for those people, thank you for my children, thank you for this wonderful, glorious life, and, yes, even thank you for my troubles."

"God, I haven't been very worthy of you. I have been treating you just like I always treated dad and Harold —

loving you when you do what I want and spitting poisonous venom at you when you don't. I'm sorry.''

Back to Eric and Brian. I think, "God, I will never be the person I would like to be, or the mother I think I should be, but with your help maybe I will be adequate."

The curtain has lifted to let warm sunshine spill into the corners of a dark room. "Let go and let God" doesn't mean getting up twenty times to check on a locked door, or shivering cowardly in my covers; nor does it mean trying to control everyone and everything that touches my life. I think of the strong metal leash I keep around the necks of Brian and Eric, never allowing them to experience failure or pain, over-protecting, smothering them. I wonder out loud if one day at a time can be broken down to mean one thing at a time.

I search through drawers looking for pencil and paper before I can lose my thought. I want to make a list, "Damn, I can't find a pencil. Got to have a pencil!" Dump out the drawer on the table, ah there's a stub, now for the list. First, lock the door once, go to bed, and let God keep out the boogeyman. Next, give up "poor little me." She had her day. Third, look for ways to like yourself. At this, I stop; this is almost too much; for years now I have put me down, called me names, wallowed in my failure, reveled in my unworthiness, delighted in my martyrdom, lauded myself for my sacrifices, gloried in my guilt. Elaine's words come back, "Do you think you are God?''

Catching sight of the serenity prayer on my wall, I shake my head. I've been saying it wrong; instead of "God help me to *accept the things I cannot change,*" I've been saying, "Help me to *change the things I cannot accept.*" Suddenly I am very, very tired, as I switch off the lights and find myself in total darkness for the first time in years. I snuggle into my fragrant, comforting bed, "You can do the worrying tonight, God."

Later in the week when Elaine stops by I tell her about all my resolutions and self-revelations. "Be careful," she says, "remember you sometimes take one step forward and two steps back. Come down gently; don't crash.''

Two weeks later I know what she means. It has been one of those days; my grades are slipping, I have a paper due, and this afternoon I was upbraided by a teacher who thinks that women with children have no business being in school. To make matters worse Eric is sick and I have no money for medicine. "Oh, Elaine, you said two, not ten.''

Momentarily I slip back into my self-reviling ways. Sternly I give myself a mental shake, "Stop it! You can pull up your grades with a little work and the teacher was showing his own stupidity, not yours, and as far as Eric is concerned, you will just have to pray for guidance and strength.''

As Eric gets sicker and sicker and I sell all the possessions I can spare to buy medicine, I say, "God, please don't do this. I will die if anything happens to Eric. Then "God, if you have to take him, please give me the strength to handle it.'' When a specialist looks at Eric and says there is nothing wrong with him that can't be cured by removal of his tonsils, I say, "Thank you, God, I will never doubt you again!'' But, of course, I do.

Twenty-nine

Why? Why? Why is it that I am only attracted to men who treat me badly? I have nothing but disdain for most of them anyway. If they like me, I wonder what is wrong with them; and if they don't, I bend and twist like a pretzel until they do like me, and then I kick them in the teeth. Will I ever, ever understand me, I wonder, as I think of my relationship with Bill? We have been going together for over a year now, not exclusively, but he is my only lover.

I think I am in love with Bill. He is tall, slim, and exotic looking. He is witty, intelligent, and supercool. He is fun and he's kind, most of the time. That is what is bothering me. For some unexplainable reason, we seem to bring out the beast in each other. Fight, fight, fight, snipe, snipe, snipe, break-up, make-up. My firmest resolve to say "It's over" gets lost like a shout in the wind as I let him interrupt me day and night. I interrupt him too. "Help, my car won't start; help, my faucet is leaking; help, help, help."

I find myself slipping, seeing the same things in Bill as I saw in Harold, trying to force Bill to be what I want him to be. "Will you never learn?" I ask myself. "Oh, leave me alone," I mutter to myself.

With as much courage as I can muster, I say, "It's all or nothing." Bill opts for nothing, but he still calls and I still call.

Thirty

Darkness is descending around us like a warm fluffy blanket when I exhaustedly flop down on my front steps. As I lean comfortably against the solidness of my house, I feel the hard coolness of the concrete beneath me. I am surrounded by the dusky night and sounds of laughter, shouts, the sound of a bat against a ball.

"Come on, mom," Brian shouts. "Get off your duff."

"Yeah, come on, mom," somebody else chimes in.

"Have a heart, you guys, we've been playing for three hours, and besides we can't see the ball."

On many evenings the boys and I got outside with the bat and ball.

Tonight as we started to play, Sue drove up. Then the next door neighbors came over, and finally the college kids lolling on the grass across the street joined in. "What's the matter, mom, you getting old?" somebody taunts.

That does it! I grab a handful of ice from my tea glass and go after the culprit. As the ice goes down the back of his neck, the ball game turns into a full fledged wrestling match on the fragrant, grassy turf. People are tumbling and shouting, gasping and shrieking. My victim is now my assailant and Eric runs in to protect me.

"Enough, enough," I gasp. People are flopped all over the

grass like discarded rag dolls as Sue and I go in the house to replenish the tea supply. When I step out the door, I hear a chorus of "Surprise!" as the kids from across the street make a great show of presenting me with an armful of misty, scented lilacs.

Everyone is gone. The boys are settled for the night and I am soaking, happily exhausted in a tub full of warm, sweet bubbles, thinking of the pleasure of simple things: ball games, picnics, swimming, and horseback riding; snowballs, sledding, hot chocolate, and Scrabble; lilacs, sunsets, strawberries, and corn on the cob. Who could doubt the wonder of life or the existence of God?

Later that night as I am dozing off, the phone beside my bed rings. It is a new friend who has joined Al-anon only recently. She suffers for a while, then begins to cry. "It's o.k.," I say, when she apologizes for her tears. "Would you like to come over?" I ask.

"No, I just need somebody to talk to," she says forlornly, mentioning tranquilizers, suicide, and God all in the same breath. She is practically telling my story. I see in her my own self-pitying, destructive behavior. She makes her accusations against everyone and everything, and says, "if only" about a dozen times. In her voice I hear myself and I tell her so. I want to comfort her, I wish I could. I feel helpless while I listen, and the only thing I can do when she finally lets up about an hour later is to tell her to take it easy and get out her Al-anon book. Together we recite the serenity prayer before she hangs up.

"God, that phone call was no accident. You wanted me to see what I sound like. Okay, I see enough all ready." I can't get back the pleasant feeling, though, as I lie there thinking how much I personally contribute to my own unhappiness, how well I rationalize and how bitter I feel about what I have been through. "Oh yeah," a little voice says, "How much of it did you bring on yourself?" Thinking of Bill, I know I practically gave him a written invitation to use me and take me for granted. What is my excuse for that one?

Thirty-one

Stealthily I reach for the phone, dialing as quietly as possible. Barely able to get air past the heart lodged in my throat, I whisper, "Sue, somebody is breaking into my house."

"Hello, Hello," she says sleepily, "I can't hear you."

"Sue," urgently now, "someone is breaking in my window." Just then I hear another muffled grating sound; tinny thumps like wood against metal screens.

"Get up and look," she says.

"I can't, I'm petrified."

Resignation, "Okay, lie still, I will be right there."

Minutes in terrifying suspense seem like hours. Soon, I hear the car pull up and the car door slam. I slip out of bed and run for the door. Sue rushes in and we hear the noise again. She goes immediately to its source and there in the dining room, by the window, caught between the wall and the space heater is a big fat mouse in a trap, jumping and squirming, banging first into the wall, then into the stove, desperately struggling for freedom. She disposes of it because I am too squeamish. It's 3:00 a.m. Over a cup of coffee she says, "You will never know how close I came to bringing the cops out with me." The image of a cop rushing in with club drawn to conquer a mouse makes us squeal with laughter.

Dawn is creeping up to the edge of the road when Sue leaves. She is such a good friend. We have shared many things: each other's kids, each other's money, each other's love life. She understands when I cry in a movie that isn't sad and laugh in a movie that isn't funny. We've pulled some dumb stunts together, like laughing uncontrollably in class, letting air out of her boyfriend's tires (when he went with another girl), and trying to get a suntan in the rain.

Sue is the one who happened to be present the very first time I told Harold, "I'm sorry, but I don't intend to listen to this," and hung up on one of his drunken tirades. Sue baked me a cake to celebrate the day I conquered my fear and filed charges against Harold for non-support. Sue understands my ambivalent feelings about Bill. I never thought it possible to share as much love with another woman as I do with Sue and Elaine. Even Bev. As much as I love her, we never leveled with each other.

Thirty-two

A classmate named John and I are sitting in the college hang-out for senior citizens, having a drink and discussing the merits of a night class we just left, and a test that is coming up. Bill comes in drunk and obnoxious. He makes loud remarks which are aimed at me and presents a great show of affection for another woman. Seeing that he cannot get my attention in that way, he comes over and twists my wrist, dragging me over to a booth to talk. "What do you want from me?" he demands spitting out insults and cutting remarks. "Do you want to get married, is that what you want?"

Head down and embarrassed I say, "I don't know, Bill."

"Then come with me and let's talk it over."

I watch as he collects the key to a friend's apartment, but when we get there we don't talk much, we make love.

Sitting now, fully dressed, contemplating his naked body lying passed out on the bed, I say, "Is this what you want for yourself? Are you crazy? Are you going to settle again for this kind of life?" No, I say as I put on my coat and gloves. "No!" I say as I methodically gather up his clothes discarded and empty as a cast off shell. No, I say when I carry them out to his car. Surreptitiously checking to make sure he is still asleep, I take his car keys, throw them on the front seat where he can see them and lock the car doors. In my own car, backing quietly out of the driveway through the misty darkness, I begin to laugh. The closer I get toward home, the harder I laugh. I am laughing so hard my body is shaking and tears are streaming down my cheeks. If a cop stops me, he will lock me up in the crazy house and throw away the key. In my bed, I laugh until I am sick to my stomach.

The next morning I am prim and proper as I sit behind a table alone in the student union. I see Bill coming down the stairs, legs akimbo like a bowlegged jockey. Before he hits the bottom stair, I am laughing. The closer he gets, the harder I laugh, trying in vain to cut it off, because people are looking at me, this prim and proper woman, sitting alone hugging her stomach in hysterical laughter.

Bill's face is purple with rage. He resolutely walks directly to my table. "Stop it!" he demands. I try, it's useless. "It's not funny, you know. I had to answer the door in a blanket." Fresh squeals burst from my mouth. "And I had to break my car window, wrapped in a bedspread with the whole town driving by." A moment of contrition is cut short by renewed howls. "Goddammit, stop laughing. What in the hell did you do with my underwear?" By now his mouth is turning up at the corners and his eyes twinkling with contained mirth as he tries to maintain his anger. We have the attention of everyone in the room and I don't even care. So much for dignity and pride.

I go to class still chuckling, trying to gain composure before the instructor comes in. That day for the first time I argue a point with a lofty professor who had always sent me cowering to the door.

John overtakes me on campus. "Remind me never to make you mad," he says. I don't try to tell him I didn't do it because I was mad. When the symbolism of it escapes me, how can I explain it to him?

When I tell them at the Al-anon meeting, they roll in the aisles. "Who, who?" they gasp. The name is not important. What is important is that I have declared my independence. The congratulations are profuse.

Thirty-three

Standing in front of my full length mirror, wearing clothes I have borrowed from my mother, I get that funny feeling again. It is strange and creepy, but sometimes I can't tell if I am me or my mother. It is an indescribable feeling that comes over me sometimes that leaves me disoriented and shaken. The mirror reflects an image that is the same size as my mother, the same build, the same stance, the same mouth, the same eyes; if I squint my eyes narrowing my vision to a haze, I can see my mother staring at me from my mirror. My reveries are interrupted by Elaine coming in the back door. "Where is your mother?" I hear her say to Eric. Eric is lost in his drawing pad in absorbed concentration. I stick my head out the bedroom door and say, "Elaine, in here."

Winding her way through the comfortable clutter of my living room, she comes. "Elaine, when you look at me, what do you see?"

Elaine doesn't know what it is I need to hear. Slowly she says, "I see a very attractive woman about five feet one inch tall, with a smart pantsuit on."

"What else do you see?" I press.

"Well, what else is there to see?"

"Elaine, you've met my mother. Do I look like her?"

"Well, yes, some."

"Do you know that when I put my mother's clothes on, I think I change into her?" She just looks at me. She has no answer for this one. A light clicks on in my head. "Elaine, you know I just realized how much Harold is like my dad. Do you know that all my life I've lived with the problems caused by someone else's drinking. Elaine, is drinking the way they did really alcoholism?"

At that I sink down on my bed, my eyes pleading with her to say I am being ridiculous. It's one thing to say Harold is probably an alcoholic, and it is quite another to slander a dead man whom I loved and hated so ferociously. She sits beside me with an arm around my shoulders. "Yes, I think that's possible." I have never told Elaine much about dad, having always focused all my bitterness on Harold; but I have discovered that Al-anon people know a lot more than I think they do.

"Elaine, do you know that I have forgiven Harold, but that I have never forgiven my dad."

"Well, now maybe you can begin to," she says. "But you want to remember that choosing to consider yourself a co-alcoholic does not give you the right to label them. Only Harold can call himself that — if he wants to. And your father is dead. Let him rest in peace."

Later that week, I am driving the few hundred miles home to visit my mother for a holiday. I mull over that conversation in my mind. Brian and Eric are sound asleep. I am all alone in friendly darkness disturbed only by occasional headlights from on-coming cars. The radio is playing soft music. "Dad, if only I had known the torture and pain you were suffering. If only I'd understood." I stare out at the ribbon of light guiding me over the blank expanse of road. Out loud I say, "Wherever you are, dad, I understand your illness was not your fault."

Brian stirs, "What, mom?"

"Nothing, Brian, I was just talking to your grandfather."

"Umm," he says sleepily snuggling against my shoulder.

The rest of the way home I think about this thing with my mother's clothes. Boy, I really did it! I emulated her so much I never had any identity of my own. I did what she did, thought what she thought, and looked to her for direction. I wish I could tell her that I just found out my dad was probably not responsible for all his drinking, that he was even sicker than we thought. It is a weird thing to find out that I have never had my own identity and that my actions have more often been reactions. I would like to share this with her, but how can I explain in one weekend what it has taken me three years to learn. I think of all the college functions I have attended, wearing men like badges. I didn't care about them, I needed them to validate my existence. I think of Bill. Yes, I loved him, but did I love him because of the perversity he brought out in me? The question is too big to answer. "Don't try, just think of him as a nice guy with a problem; not one you caused and not one you have to deal with."

I think of all the things I have learned in Al-anon, some of them painful, such as the way alcoholism affects the whole family. I thought my brothers were perfect. I idolized them with the blind adoration reserved for those who hold the key to life's mysterious formula. "How," I used to ask myself, "can they be so smart, so cool? What is it that makes the rest of this family tick? Why were they born with a special something that I am not allowed to possess?" Now I see that each of us searched for and found our own particular way of survival amid alcoholism.

Stuart was quiet, introverted, hard as nails with a seething anger smoking under his nice guy front. Ted and Michael were smooth, selfishly shrewd, daring intellectuals who would allow themselves no weaknesses or lack of perfection. Bernie was the family hero, the too-good-to-be-true guy that everybody longs to have for a husband, son, or brother.

All of us were angry, rebellious, hiding behind a toughness, lest we should reveal the effects of alcoholism, the incredible family weakness, not even discussing with each other this unspeakable thing of shame. Each of us, with our deep seated guilt, our feeling of unworthiness, and our contempt for fallibility, coped with life in the way that we found best protected us.

I have learned a great deal about alcoholism. Like a hungry cancer, the fears, feelings, and pain ripple and spread, stretching to touch and affect all who come in contact with the alcoholic. Spouse, children, and friends, aunts, uncles and cousins, grandchildren and even great grandchildren — all are affected, until someday, sometime, someone chooses to get off the circle and find a different path.

Today, I wonder how many people die never knowing or understanding how they have been victimized by alcoholism. How many people, like me, will thrash blindly through a thicket of pain rather than tackle the unknown or admit to needing help?

Do other people have as much trouble facing reality as I did? Yes, I know they do; my Al-anon group is proof of that. I have much to do yet, but —

"I'm learning; boy, am I learning," I mutter as I think of how I have conquered my fear of the dark, and how I now fix my own faucets, or call a repairman. I have even forced myself to let go a little of Brian and Eric, no longer wringing my hands in guilt for what they had to go through, no longer fearing for their safety everytime they step out the door. Even finding the strength to tell them things about their father that they can be proud of, recreating for them some of the happy times. Now they are allowed to visit him from time to time, not without some fear, but saying, "If it be your will, God, let them have a nice, sober weekend, and let them return safely." Overprotective? Yes. Possessive? Yes. But learning.

In my mother's home, after the hello, the hugs, and the kisses, over coffee I try to tell her some of the things on my mind. She is very sensitive on the subject of dad, but often talks of her loneliness and sometimes her guilt for some of the things he was. This time I say, "That's nonsense, mother. It's not your fault. Dad had some problems but you did the best you could." To my surprise she accepts this.

On my way back to school, I think about mom and dad. Where is it written that I have to choose between them? Why did I think that I need to be like one or the other? Why not take the best of both and just be me? I send a little prayer God's way saying "Thank you for the revelation, Lord. Please take the new me and use my talents in whatever way you see fit, but make the messages plain, God. Sometimes I have to be hit over the head." I realize with a little flash of guilt that it has been months since I have thought of Bernie. Without my even knowing it, the grief has eased away. "Guess what, Bernie," I say, "I am somebody." Then I say it again slowly, "I AM SOMEBODY."

Thirty-four

Elaine is moving away. As I help her pack, we crack jokes and laugh, occasionally lapsing into sadness.

Elaine's friendship is an indisputable godsend. She stood by me while my befuddled mind mucked around in abstract confusion, but I found myself being able to give a lot to her, too. The dam behind my eyes is threatening to break into gushing torrents as we lug boxes out to a trailer and survey the now topsy-turvy half-empty house. The walls look bare and forlorn, the windows naked. I don't want to make it any harder for her to go by being tearful and sentimental but I want to say something. "Elaine," I say, "be happy. I am going to miss you, but I . . . I want you to know . . . ."

"Oh, cut the corn," she says turning swiftly to hide her eyes. It's o.k. We both know life can't stand still. The comforting thing is that wherever and whenever we meet again, there will be instant heart to heart communication, none of this "How are you? I am fine" trivia.

I have some bad moments when I return home from Elaine's now empty house. So I indulge myself in sadness and have a good cry.

It is all right, I think, to cry when you are sad. I have

controlled my emotions for so many years that I doubt it will ever be possible for me to be completely spontaneous, but I am getting better at it.

The other day, I instinctively hugged a teacher, when I learned I'd received an A. She shook me off uncomfortably and I walked away thinking "Thank God that's her hangup, not mine."

The meaning of detachment is coming to me in bits and pieces. The latest insight is that I have the ability to choose my attitude, and I have the ability to let those I love live their own lives without my interference.

Thirty-five

The boys are outside playing and I am comfortably sprawled on a sagging couch in my living room, trying to study. It's hard to study on lazy Sunday afternoons because I keep getting lost in thought. I think of the peacefulness of my mind and body as I reflect on how far I have come since that terrible time when it was necessary to constantly fight and scratch and flee.

With God's help and the help of loving friends, my welfare worker who had the wisdom to force me to shed my false pride, my true friends who refused me the dodge of lying to myself, my professor who insisted on quality work, I have learned the real meanings of pride and dignity. They are not taught, they are earned.

I am beginning to see a pattern. Harold wasn't the only one who didn't take responsibility for his actions. I used the whole world as a scapegoat. When I was little, I blamed my mother for my dad's actions, thinking that if she would only under- stand him, he wouldn't do the things he did. When I got older, I blamed my father for my miserable life. After all, would I ever have behaved the way I did — rushing to get married if it weren't for him?

Finally, almost everything bad that ever happened in our marriage was Harold's fault. Even my friends came in for their share of the blame. I giggle at the mental image of a puppet who looks like me. "Here she is, folks. Pull a string, push a button, what comes out is up to you." I see that blaming is a habit that won't break easily. I must really work at taking the responsibility for my own actions and owning up to my own feelings.

There are some things about myself I must accept and work around. For instance, my ability to leap a tall mud puddle with a single bound and land in the middle with a splat. I know I must not wallow in it, but crawl out. My ability to lie to myself and rationalize my way into thinking that I have personal control over my life or anyone else's. I have learned that the best friends are those who love me enough to tell me things I don't want to hear, and I am accepting that life is a constant process of learning, giving, sharing, and taking. I know God loves me very much to have waited so patiently while I muddled around with my pride and self-pity.

Funny how I had the idea that I was the only one in the world that life had dealt some near fatal blows. I was even sort of proud of it in a perverse way. Everywhere I looked I saw others like me. But I didn't want to see them. I needed some claim to fame. That's why I got such horrible headaches when I was going to group, and later when I went to Al-anon, I didn't want to listen to their problems. I wanted them to hear mine. And then I wanted them to tell me how wonderfully patient and kind I am. I certainly didn't care to hear that I could be anything short of perfect. After all, look what I'd put up with. It came as quite a shock to me that many of the good things I had done weren't really good at all but selfish ways to maintain control over another human being.

The first time I heard the word co-alcoholic it made me angry. The first time I had to say I was one, I choked over the words. Now I can say it simply and easily, accepting it as a term that means I've experienced many problems in my life from alcohol. The saying is "once an alcoholic always an alcoholic" and I believe that to be true of co-alcoholics also. Therefore, I must guard against my tendency to fall back into my old self-defeating ways of control and self-pity, and I must work toward my goal of caring for myself in a constructive way. Eric interrupts my reveries, tugging on my sleeve, "Mom, I'm hungry, when are we going to eat?"

"Eric, how would you like to fix supper?"

"Me?" His little face beams with delight, "Okay, mom, you stay in here, don't come out 'til I call you."

Later Brian and I sample crusty black tinged pizza and lumpy scrambled eggs while Eric hovers and beams. I shake my head at Brian as he opens his mouth to give his brotherly comments and he winks at me as he offers to help clean up the dripping egg yolk and the smoking pans. I am struck with pure joy in my family and in my life.

It is a strange world, this. Now that I refuse to play games, everyone thinks I am playing games. People who thought I was being open and honest when I was manipulating them now think I am manipulating them when I am being open and honest. Tonight I experienced a real triumph. I went to a college party alone. I had known about the party for weeks. The old me would have broken her neck to get a date, and failing that, stayed home cursing her ugliness. The new me decided if someone asked me, fine: if not, I would go alone. This resolution was almost broken when a friend (and I use the term loosely) called to say she was going to the party with Arnie, a man I am presently dating. She happens to be from my Al-anon group. I'd expected more loyalty than that. "Well, what do you expect?" I ask myself, "Al-anon people are only human, and probably more human than most." I decide to react by not reacting and sincerely wished her well.

Anyway, tonight, I did it. I walked into a crowded room, comprised of mostly laughing, happy couples and stifling my doubts about this move, I joined a group at a large table in the middle, near the dance floor. I did not sit with Sue and her date. That would be too easy. A lot of unattached males are holding up the wall around the dimly lit room, and suddenly I find I am dancing every dance. The absolute corker is when Arnie and I are dancing and he angrily demands to know what I am trying to prove.

Oh, Arnie, if only I could make you believe that all I am trying to prove is my ability to function as a whole complete person.

"Are you trying to make me look like a heel, coming out here alone?"

"No, Arnie," I say, "this has nothing to do with you." I don't even crow when the look on his date's face changes from one of smugness to envy. Oh, it is a strange world all right: wonderful, but strange.

People find the new me a little difficult to deal with at times. Some consider my relaxed attitude and directness insufferable. Like the other night when I was leaving the library. Bob was coming out of the door at the same time. "Can I buy you a cup of coffee?" he asked.

"I can't, I have to get home. The kids are alone, but I will make you one if you like."

The house was silent. The kids were asleep. I flipped on the radio and filled the coffee pot with water. As I reached up in the cupboard for the coffee, two arms came around me from behind cupping my breasts. Bob had pulled this on me before; formerly I apologetically squirmed away from his advances, pretending not to know what was on his mind. This time, I stopped what I was doing, slowly and deliberately dumping the water out of the coffee pot before I turned to face him. "Look, Bob," I said looking him squarely in the eye, "I am getting very tired of hearing sex called coffee. If you want sex, why don't you just say how about a roll in the hay, and then I can say no and save us both some time." He backed out of my kitchen door slinging epithets consisting mostly of "You're a loser, a waste of time." But I knew better; I know I was a winner.

Confidence is lovely, confidence is great, but a little fear is healthy, I tell myself. I am waiting to be introduced as a speaker for our co-ed toastmaster club. Swallowing hard, I glance around the room. "Come on, they are just classmates, you've done this before. Knees, will you please quit knocking." When it's over, I have the trophy for giving the best ten-minute speech.

The name of my speech was *How To Fight The Clean Fight*. I had set the stage in advance, briefing the toastmaster and telling him to introduce me in an uncomplimentary way. When he did, I let him have it with a verbal barrage, telling him I ate little boys like him for breakfast; then I wound my way up to the front of the room amidst astonished gasps, followed by an embarrassed hush.

"Fellow Toastmasters, Ladies and Gentlemen," I begin, "what you have just seen is a demonstration of how NOT to fight." Audible signs of relief permeated the air as I launched into "cup filling," "hitting below the belt" and "straight messages."

Brian and Eric were waiting up for me when I majestically swept in with my prize. Their congratulations were profuse. "Thanks, guys," I said, "it was nothing." They knew I was kidding and a great discussion ensued over where we were going to display the "nothing."

A big dividend in my new way of life is the subtle change in our atmosphere at home. The boys and I no longer cling together for survival but have a sincere enjoyment in each other's company. I have missed a lot of boats where they are concerned, but that is behind us. We are back in church and Sunday School. We occasionally use the good china and salad forks just for us. When we can manage it, we go out to dinner, just the three of us, really enjoying our discussion of the events of the day or the latest happenings. I can never tell them all I have learned. I can only show by example, and hope they can pick up for themselves. Their cooperative change in attitude leaves me breathless sometimes, and I know Brian saw the tears in my eyes the other night when he changed his attitude from "When I get to be sixteen, I am going to quit school" to "mom, when I get to college . . . " and then a little defensively, "Well, a guy can change his mind, can't he?"

"Yes, Brian, a guy certainly can."

Brian is going through a phase. I find it amusing and a little disconcerting. He is hosting the weekly meeting of his 4-H club tonight. Everything is in readiness, exactly the way he wants it. I am in my bedroom getting dressed; he comes in, plops on the bed, looks at me and moans, "Oh, mother, you don't look like a mother."

"Brian," I say, "this is the most motherly dress I own. What is wrong with it?" I point out long sleeves, highneck, modest hemline.

"Why do you have to wear a dress at all? Why can't you wear your jeans? At least mess-up your hair, so you will look like the other mothers." I have heard of kids being ashamed of their mothers, but this is ridiculous. My compromise is an apron.

Brian is going to his first junior high dance. He asks me to drive him to the high school. We are driving down the street. Suddenly he lets out an agonized groan and slips to the floor, "Cut through that alley, quick!" he says urgently. "Are we in the alley yet?"

"Yes, Brian."

"O.K.," he says, sliding from the depths of the space under the glove compartment, "I'll get out here."

I understand his embarrassment at being caught driven to the dance by his mother. "Who is she, Brian?" I ask.

For a brief instant his face reddens in surprise, then he says, "Oh, just some dumb old girl."

When Brian is troubled, he follows me around the house going from room to room wherever I am. It is when he picks up the dish towel and begins to dry the dishes without being asked that I know he has real problems. "Do you want to talk about it, Brian?" I ask.

"About what?" he says morosely.

"About whatever is bothering you." When we finish discussing this particular problem, he looks as if he just has been relieved of the weight of the world. "Thanks, mom," he says throwing down his towel and heading out the door. Then sticking his head back in the door, he says, "Since you want to be a counselor, I thought I would give you some practice."

"The pleasure is all mine, Brian." I say. "Now come back here and finish the dishes." He does, grinning all the while and snapping me with the towel.

Brian and Eric tell me that the kids in school give them a bad time because they don't have a father. "But you do have a father," I say.

"Oh, mom, you don't understand."

"Well, I would really like to," I say, "but you're right, I don't." I feel so helpless when they tell me things like that. But what I usually end up saying is, "It's an imperfect world and you have to learn to cope. What are some of the ways you can deal with this?" They usually manage to come up with solutions that are satisfactory to them.

Eric has a lot of emotional problems. I've talked to the doctor about this, and he tells me it is not at all unusual for a child who has had spinal meningitis to have these aftereffects. I wish I could blame it all on that, but I know I can't.

Eric is superintelligent and school bores him to death. His vocabulary is better than most adults and he is the delight of most grown-ups, but a hair-tearing problem to his teachers. No provisions are made to challenge his inquiring mind and his classroom antics have me on the carpet about once a month.

At age six, Eric is sometimes a lost little boy, sometimes a pure, innocent delight. He thinks deep and dreams expansive dreams. He often sees right through to the heart of a situation and makes flat statements that can bring me down to earth in a hurry and confront me with annoying truths. He loves long discussions about family, friends, and religion. At this particular moment we are talking about his father and why he doesn't come to see him more often. Trying to ease his feelings, I say, "He's busy among other things. Looking me in the eye, he says, "Busy drinking, mom, and that's no excuse."

Out of the mouths of babes, I think. No, there is no fooling Eric. I wish for him to never have to know stifled creativity and the smothering of a mask. But already he is being molded into "another classroom face" conformity.

I feel a tug on my hand, a weight hits my bed. Struggling to gain consciousness from a far-off cloud, I try to open my eyes. Open one eye — through a haze see Brian and Eric, arms full of — struggle harder. "Surprise! Happy Mother's Day!" The smell of bacon and eggs sifts up my nose. Sleepily, I push myself up on one elbow. There is Eric with the packages, Brian with the breakfast. They are excited and happy. A glance at my watch tells me it is 6:00 a.m. Both the breakfast and the packages settle in my lap, and bodies crawl up beside me to watch in anticipation. First the box with the red ribbon — a candy dish peeks out at me from its thorny bed of shredded newspaper. "It's just what I wanted! Thank you!"

"Open the other one — no, wait, guess."

"I can't guess, I am too excited."

"Me, too," Eric says as he starts to help me rip off the paper. The box is open; staring me in the face is a pair of white shoes. "Oh," I say as the tears hit my eyes, "Oh, how did you know?"

"Mother," Brian says exasperatedly, "don't cry. Are they the right size? Will they fit?"

"How . . . " I say, "Where . . . ?" I blubber. It is hard to believe how important a pair of shoes can be to someone who must guard every penny.

"Those are the ones you were looking at in the window, aren't they?"

"Oh, yes, they are; oh, thank you." I try to give them hugs but they are too anxious to see me eat my breakfast. I choke down as much cold egg and greasy bacon as I can while their eyes follow every bite from plate to mouth.

Give me Cadillacs, give me mink coats, nothing can rival the pride and happiness I feel as I sit later in church, staring down at my new shoes thinking how they must have saved and planned for this day. When the moment for silent prayer comes, I thank God for the gift of life, for the direction in which he is steering us. I am bursting with pride for the children standing beside me who have learned to make sacrifices for love and who, I hope, are also learning that sacrifice is only one fraction of love and that caring for yourself is the other. I think of how Harold actually forced me to be strong with his, "You can handle it, babe" and how I did him no favors by not saying, "So can you." It's hard for me to let my kids make their own mistakes, hard to stand by and let them fall sometimes, but I know I must.

Thirty-six

Yesterday I was pleased and happy when I was informed that I had been selected to work as an intern to do counseling in the mental health ward of a government hospital. I applied several weeks ago and had tried not to give it much thought while I waited for the answer.

Today I am scared to death. I didn't know I was going to do it. I thought I was going to observe, at least for awhile, but when I reported to the head counselor this morning, he took me down a long corridor. I glanced around myself nervously and with regret as I followed him, noting that the nurses' station was getting farther and farther away. Opening a door he says, "Here's your office, here is your tape recorder, and here is my phone number if anything happens you can't handle." As he opens the door to leave again, he says, "Your first patient will be in shortly."

Panic stricken, I glance around the office which is plain and nondescript, the furniture ugly government issue. A couch climbs the wall on one side and a hard wooden captain's chair faces the desk. What the hell am I doing here anyway?

The nurse opens the door and introduces me to my first client. I am on my own as he takes the unyielding wooden chair. He leans forward gripping the chair arms, his knuckles turning white.

"Relax," I say, "I am just as nervous as you are."

His knuckles loosen, he leans back a little and says defiantly, "What do you want from me?" This is a good question because I don't know, but I do know we can't sit here and stare at each other for an hour. I say, "What I would really like is to get to know you."

He talks stiltedly, fidgeting uncomfortably at first, but finally begins to relax as the hour comes to an end. I am weak with relief when the door closes behind him. Another first!

I go to the hospital three times a week for a year. I help with group sessions, sometimes I play pool or go for walks with patients. I have my own case load and I have picked up on the fact that two of my patients are alcoholics. One patient in particular grabs my heart strings, and I fight with my supervisor over the medication and shock treatments he is being given. In my heart I am sure he should be treated for alcoholism. I find myself spending my own time on Saturday working with him and his children. I will never know what happened to him, but I am able to affect the lives of his two children, using the Al-anon concepts. His teenage daughter calls me one day to thank me and I feel very humble.

I am beginning to feel a rapport with the world that I didn't think could ever exist for me. Not worrying about what could happen, not dwelling on what might break down, blow up, or conk out, not giving in to the frustrations of petty things leaves with me a lot more energy than I have had for years.

The kids and I are going roller skating one Sunday afternoon. "Just one session, guys," I say, "that's all we can afford today."

"Mom," Eric says, "are we poor?"

"If you mean do we have any money, Eric, the answer is no, but we are rich in all the ways that count."

A friend of mine was killed in a car accident. Her life snuffed out so quickly, so easily by a combination of machine, booze, and pills. I went to her funeral today and cried first for the waste of life and then for me. I sit now in my warm cozy kitchen, contemplating the raindrops on my crying windows. I wonder about death and try to decide whether or not I want to be alone. Once I had no choice; I was alone even when I was with people. Now I know I have only to pick up the phone, and someone will come.

My friend's mother didn't even cry. Everyone said, "Isn't she holding up well? See how composed she is; isn't that something?"

I didn't think she was something at all. If you love somebody, you could at least stop thinking about your image long enough to cry for them. Yet, as I think this over, I know I would have agreed with them a couple of years ago.

I hear Brian and Eric playing in their bedroom — sounds like the whole neighborhood is in there. The sounds are comforting. I think of my friend's children who now have no mother. I am very sorry for them. I think of my children who deserve more than I have ever given them, and guilt washes over me like a foaming, roaring tidal wave.

I can sit here and say ignorance may have been a good excuse once, but it is not anymore. It's time to face life without excuses, time to put the blame right where it belongs, time to take a look at what is happening. I know I am better, I know I am growing, yet the pain of my contribution to their pain will not be easily dispelled. The bedroom door pops open, a half-dozen small bodies tumble out. "Come see our forts. Can we have some cookies? Aw, it's still raining."

"Quiet, guys," I say, "I'm thinking."

"Mom, you gotta see this," Eric is pulling on one hand, Brian on the other.

"Okay, I give up."

Out of chairs and blankets, they have fashioned protective shelters from which they can shoot spitwads and popcorn. I try not to see the mess, and concentrating on the ingenious "forts," I say, "Looks like a lot of fun. You guys are pretty clever."

They continue to play; I continue to think. I decide my grief is not only for my friend, but for everyone that suffers the pain of trying to cope in this strange, strange world. I feel guilt at having dropped this friend because of her booze and drugs. Now I wonder, could I have done anything, said anything? Maybe, maybe not. I certainly don't need to add this to my other burdens.

I have to stop and remember that I am not responsible for the sins of the world. I have no control over anyone else's life and not much over my own. I have only choices. I chose to stay away from this friend because my own health depended on not getting on her merry-go-round. She was a woman in pain, the pain of being beaten periodically by a macho he-man. The pain of being a failure in a world that says women can control what happens in their homes, the pain of constant searching for the "happy ever after." She chose her escape without benefit of counsel. The tired, well-worn phrase goes through my mind as I resolve to let her passing be an inspiration to me, "There but for the grace of God go I."

Sometime ago, I was nominated to be the public relations officer for the college English club. As such I am also the coordinator and master of ceremonies for the annual spring banquet. What a challenge! Night after night, the entertainment committee sits at my kitchen table and we plan. We decide to do a mock award ceremony and spend hour after hour, laughing, banging our fists on the table, almost falling off our chairs with exuberant, belly shaking laughter. "Would we dare to give the club loudmouth a trophy that says 'World's Greatest Bull Artist'? No, better not. Let's give it to the quiet guy who never says anything."

"How about Angie? Will she be hurt or pleased if we give her this ugly purple troll with the head bobbing up and down that says, "We deserve each other?" Yeah, Angie is a good sport; she can take it."

On and on we plan, we shop for doo dads, knick knacks,

and gewgaws. The hours we spend in excited merriment cannot possibly be topped by the banquet itself.

By now I often attend functions alone, by choice. I have discovered I sometimes meet the most interesting people if not hampered by a partner. As master of ceremonies tonight, I must arrive early to see that things go smoothly. A mile from the club where we are holding this event, my car skids, flaps and flops as the back tire gives up the ghost. Down the highway I float in my borrowed cream colored floor length formal, my gold slippers clipping merrily along. One of the other club members stops for me and kids me, saying, "You didn't have to go to such great lengths to ride with me." "Oh, damn, you mean I stuck that nail in there for nothing?"

At the banquet I see to the comfort of the guest speaker and then it is zero hour.

Standing behind the podium, looking out at the sea of hundred faces, I calmly begin the welcome and introductions.

As I listen to the speaker, a note is winding its way up the other end of the table. The note says, "Careful, your serenity is showing. Love, Sue." The mini-awards are a rolling success, each one chosen to represent a loved idiosyncrasy of its receiver. The last one presented is a gigantic bottle of Mr. Clean which goes with much affection to our club president who is always telling us to clean up our act.

Later, when a friend takes me to my car, we are discussing the fine art of being happy. He says to me, "How is it that you are always so up?"

"Because," I say, "for the first time in my life, I am free."

"You mean, you really like being divorced?" he asks.

"It's a lot deeper than that. Actually it doesn't have anything to do with divorce. I mean free in the sense of being among the living."

He smiles a tolerant smile and says, "You're really lucky." Lucky? "Yes, I suppose you could call it luck."

Thirty-seven

Over the sounds of gushing water I hear banging on the door;
there it goes again. Damn, somebody is at the door and I have
my head in the sink. "Brian, get the door please." The knock
sounds again, "Brian, where are you?" I sputter, soapy water
running in my eyes and in my mouth. Who could that be on
Saturday morning? Brian pulls himself away from the car-
toons and lazily opens the door.

"Mom, mom, it's dad!" Eric runs to greet Harold, too. I
lift my dripping head and grab a towel.

"Sit down if you like," I say to him, "it's nice to see you."

He looks a little older, a littler tireder, but then I think,
don't we all. I excuse myself to finish washing my hair.

"Babe?" Harold is standing at the kitchen door, "Can I
take the boys for a while?"

"Yes," I say, not asking my usual questions of where and
how long. They pile happily out the door and I am grateful for
the unexpected free time.

When Harold brings the boys back, they are happy,
disheveled and tired. He asks if the four of us can go out to
dinner together. The boys are saying, "Please, mom, please,
dad promised to buy us the biggest steak in town."

"Great!" I say, "Give me a minute to get ready." Once I

would have been consumed with resentment and rage at this tactic, and the result would have been tears, anger, and hard feelings.

Over dinner, as the four of us talk and crack jokes, my feeling is one of contentment, compassion, and love. Yes, love, not husband-wife love but fellow human being love. I wish with all my heart that I had understood my own illness years ago, but I didn't and I can't change that; neither could I change Harold, not then, not now, not ever.

Once I cried bloody tears for Harold's soul, and I beat on my chest like an ape in the forest, screaming for vindication. "See me, I screamed, I never did anything to deserve this! See me, see how I worked, see how I suffered, see how I sacrificed! See what he did to me!" Now I know the truth to be, *See what I did to me.*

"Can I talk to you a minute?" Harold says as we pull up in front of the house. Eric is passed out in the back seat so Harold carries him to bed, then we sit down to talk. He wants to know about the boys. I share with him what I can, reciting the things that make them each special, giving him credit where I can. "You know, Harold, it was you who taught them their good manners. The teachers are always telling me how impressed they are."

Harold must leave, it's late. He says, "Thank you, thank you, for a good day. There is something really different about you, but I don't know what it is."

"Harold," I say gently, "I have found out that I had a lot of problems that were my own making. We had a lot of good times, too, so let's try to forget the bad ones and just think about the good ones, o.k.?

"Thanks, babe," he says and walks out the door. That night I include Harold in my prayers.

As I talk my private talk with God, discussing with him the events of the day, the realization hits me. I have made my peace with Him and truly feel his divine guidance in my life. I have accepted my early years as something that happened, not because I was a rotten kid, or a terrible wife, but because the whole family was in the grip of a widely misunderstood disease. It didn't happen because either dad or Harold was a loser, a weakling, or a good-for-nothing. Both possessed intelligence, morals, sensitivity, and high ideals. Both set high personal standards of perfection, and although they blamed us for their drinking, they did not drink because of me, the family, or their problems. They drank because they were alcoholics. Unfortunately, alcohol set off a deadly reaction that triggered the sinister mechanism of alcoholism in them, and we who were close to them became entwined in the problems of alcoholism, just as surely as they were, although in somewhat different ways. I do not feel any longer that dad's or Harold's treatment of me was a personal vendetta against me. The word forgiveness implies that it was, therefore it is not my place to forgive them. Accepting and understanding the disease wipes out the need to forgive.

At this moment I realize that the person I need to concern myself about forgiving is me. In all this time I still haven't forgiven me. Not rationalize, intellectualize, or excuse, but forgive. My attack of guilt at dinner made me realize that guilt can be a form of self-importance. A self-defeating tactic that still does not allow God his rightful place as Divine Controller. Is not guilt over something in which you have no control the highest form of conceit?

Lying there in the darkness, feeling at peace with the world, I say, "God, reach in and take away my guilt and let it be gone forever." In my half-conscious state, eyes closed, I see a vapor begin to rise from my breast, and it rises and rises, like an endless wispy cloud. There is pain in my chest similar to that in a hand when one wakes from stopped circulation and then feels an indescribable flooding feeling of relief. The next morning, as I think over this phenomenon, I want to run, jump, laugh, cry, and tell the whole world about God and his love. Surely, I think, my face must be lit up like the glow of a one-hundred watt bulb.

Thirty-eight

Standing by the window with my phone in my hand, I hear the dull, vibrating tones of its ringing at the other end. "Be home. Mom, please be there." The lilac bush outside my window is the first kiss of spring; the grass is sparkling like a tray of diamonds in the morning dew. "Come on, mom, answer the phone. I gotta tell you this."

A groggy, "Hello" comes from the other end. I have been up all night. I didn't realize it was so early.

"Mom, wake up, guess what?" My voice is excited.

"What?" she says instantly alert.

Hugging my news to myself for just a little longer, I say, "I am sorry I woke you up."

"It's all right, dear. What do you need?"

"Mom, I'm getting married to the most wonderful, super-fantastic guy."

She is silent. She has heard that before. Recovering quickly, she says, "That is wonderful news, dear, but who is he? What does he do?"

"It's John, mom, and it doesn't matter what he does. I am going to bring him home next weekend so you can meet him."

"If you love him, I know I will," she says.

"Oh, mom, you are a sweetheart, but what if his parents are upset?" With a momentary lapse, I say, "What will I do if they hate me, a divorcee with two children?

"Look, darling, when they meet you they will know instantly that John has picked the sweetest, most lovable girl in the world."

"Thank you, mom."

Hugging my knees to my breast, dreamily staring into space, I think of John. Funny how he came along after I had decided I liked my life just the way it is. Funny that now that I am no longer afraid, or angry, funny that now I am not only at peace with myself, but actually liking myself, there is John.

With John there were no fireworks, no loud explosions, no banners waving. With John it began as an occassional hello in classes we shared together. With John it was a cup of coffee in the cafeteria, or a friendly drink on an accidental meeting downtown. With John it was studying together for a test, it was pure friendship. When someone asked me if I had ever dated John, I said, "No, he's not my type."

The first time John asked me for a date, I went because I liked him and I had nothing else to do. The next time John asked me for a date I went because I get an indescribable feeling of harmony and tranquility in his presence. To say that being in his arms or just being near him is like being wrapped in a warm friendly cocoon is not very romantic, but that's the way it is.

Everything is different with John. There has never been any ownership. There has never been any need to call up and apologize for cutting remarks. With John it's always been you be you and I will be me. With John there was no game playing, no standing in front of the mirror making sure every hair was in place. No searching for the right thing to say. With John it is intellectual discussions, pure innocent fun, and a genuine concern for each other's needs.

"John, there are some things you need to know before we get married. I hate domesticity, housework, and gossip."

"Doesn't everybody?" he asks. That gives me the courage to tell him some other things concerning me that I think are important for him to know. As I wait to see how he will take these I give the final thrust.

"I have dedicated my life, as much of it as I can give, to helping other people, and I have asked God to use me in whatever way He sees fit. I can't say what all this will involve, or in what direction it might lead me. Can you live with that?"

The answer comes back, "I don't know. I need some time to think about it."

"I understand," I say, and I do. He has picked a woman with a purpose, not only that, but a woman with two children. One or the other might make a new marriage difficult, but the two together might make it impossible. One thing I know for sure, if the answer is no, I will be hurt but not crippled. I will cry, but I won't die. This is the first man in my life I have never tried to con, that I have never manipulated, and I honestly want what is best for him.

John takes his time to think it over and I can see the struggle going on inside of him. When he chooses to go out with another woman, I don't cry or wring my hands or beg God to send him back to me. I call a friend and go out for dinner and have a good time. When we break our engagement, I don't rush downtown to have a drink or start looking around for someone to take his place. I buy a new chair for my living room, paint my kitchen, and scrub my house within an inch of its life. In an odd sort of way, I enjoy the independence, even though I mourn the loss and miss the warmth and caring. With a calmness that comes from explicit trust in my God, I know that if God wants us to get married, we will, and if He doesn't, we won't.

Some months later when we are married, I thank God for this blessing and ask God that He "live in our home, helping us to be not one but two somebodies working together."

Graduation day dawns bright and clear. The sunshine dazzles me as I stand in line in my cap and gown, waiting outside for the march to begin. Inside are my new husband, my sons, my mother, and my brothers. Another ending, another beginning. The girl in line behind me is hugging herself with excitement, dancing around in place. "What are you going to do?" she asks me.

"Me?" I say, "I'm going to live."

She looks askance at me as the music begins and a hush falls. When I march to the front to receive my diploma, there is merriment in my eyes, confidence in my walk, and a smile on my face. I am not concerned about tomorrow, only today. Back to my seat, I bow my head a moment saying, "Thank you, God."

"Thank you for Al-Anon. Thank you, God, for helping me learn that to forgive myself is the first step to forgiving others, that to love myself is the first step to loving others, and that to accept Your wisdom is TO BE SOMEBODY."